The Story of Gigha
The Flourishing Island

by

Kathleen Philip
M.A. (Hons. Hist. Glas.)

Maps by M. T. Hart.
Drawings by M. T. Hart and F. Graham.

Published by the Author at Gigha, Gateside, Beith,
Ayrshire KA15 2 LE

Copyright the Author, 1979.
Printed by Brown Bros. (Irvine) Ltd.
ISBN 0 9501056 4 3.

i

As a token of my affectionate gratitude I dedicate **The Flourishing Island** to all my Gigha friends, both those who live on the Island and those who, like myself, are exiles.

MY WARMEST THANKS TO . . .

All the people whose cheerful enthusiasm has made this book possible.

The Staffs of the Glasgow University Library and the Scottish Record Office for the alacrity with which they have found the books and documents I required; Mr. Murdo MacDonald for his profitable searching into the Argyll Archives for Gigha material; Mr. D. W. Landale, the present Owner of Gigha for his generosity in allowing me to study the Estate papers in the relevant Office in Edinburgh where I have much appreciated the hospitality and helpfulness of the Staff.

To various authors, whom I name in the Notes, for allowing me to make use of their researches. In this connection I should like to mention especially the Kintyre Antiquarian Society and H. M. Commissioners on the Ancient and Historical Monuments of Scotland; Mrs. Judith Philip, herself a lover of Gigha, for all the valuable information she has given me; Dr. Ian Muirhead for his illuminating remarks about the Church in Scotland in the 18th Century.

The ladies who have converted my Manuscript into impeccable typing, Mrs. Reid, Mrs. Monk and Mrs. McClure; Mr. Boyle and Mike for the care they have taken so cheerfully and successfully to print and produce the volume you hold in your hand.

My friend and partner of many years standing, Miss Molly Hart, without whose continual encouragement and enthusiasm the project would not have come to fruition. She has seen to all my creature comforts, driven me on all my journeys, drawn maps and pictures and corrected proofs. In addition, and most important, she has listened to all my conversations and made valuable suggestions.

All the friends of Gigha who have helped me; Mr. McNeill Kivett of North Carolina, U.S.A. for generously sharing with me his private research into the lives of his own ancestors who lived on Gigha in the early 18th Century; Mrs. Rose McCulloch (nee Bannatyne), Mrs. Marianne Mackie (nee Andrew) and Mr. Tom Gillies for not only lending me rare books and photographs but also for allowing me to draw on their own memories of their early lives on Gigha.

Last, but by no means least, the inhabitants of the Island today, almost every one of them, from the school children to the oldest inhabitant, incomers and natives, men, women and children. To name them all here would be impossible, many I have mentioned in the text, but I feel I must especially thank Betty McNeill for zealously sharing her extensive valuable local knowledge and Margaret and Seumas McSporran for their enthusiastic co-operation, practical assistance and also for the many happy holidays I have spent in their home.

As a token of my gratitude I dedicate this book to all my Gigha friends.

Putting on a green on Gigha Golf Course, c. 1908.
Drawn by M. T. Hart from an old faded photograph taken by Charles Reid, Wishaw.

Contents

THE FLOURISHING ISLAND

Introduction

I am glad you are going to accompany me as I set out to trace the life of the people of Gigha throughout the centuries.

My story is called *The Flourishing Island* for several reasons. The Dictionary meaning of the word is ' to grow vigorously ' and no doubt at all exists that all plant life grows with vigour on Gigha. Its loveliness is beyond dispute: an Island where ' nature paints a picture no artist can excel.' Wild flowers grow in profusion, pink and blue, white and golden, Exotic plants, flaming reds and deep purples, tall Palm trees, feathery Pampas Grass as well as leafy green forest trees. On the many white sandy bays by the glass-clear sea the rocks are covered with lichen, yellow and silver grey. Among the lush green fields and easily climbed heather and bracken-covered knolls stand well-appointed cottages and modern farms.

In these cottages live men and women whose predecessors have used to good effect the natural advantages of their Island. To this less obvious, but no less vital, aspect the word flourishing applies. Until the late 18th Century we know nothing, except by inference, of the actual life of the people of Gigha but, just before the 19th Century begins, this dearth of live material is amply made up for by the wealth of contemporary documents, many of them written by eye-witnesses on Gigha itself by the light of which we can walk around the Island seeing how the people live, what they do, what their names are and, often, we can catch a glimpse of their personal lives.

Within these well-documented years times of prosperity have naturally been followed by sloughs of depression but, to me, the really extraordinary fact about Gigha is that, unlike so many other Islands, an ebb tide of life has been succeeded by a full tide of happiness. The rhythm of the tides, of the Seasons themselves, governs the historical life as they determine the daily life. Winter is not severe and Spring comes quickly to be followed by high Summer. The lush green grass dies down for a time, old families may leave the Island, former customs die out, but always the grass grows luxuriantly again, new families arrive to infuse vigorous new blood, traditional ways are adjusted to contemporary needs. A promising line of Lairds may die out to be succeeded by a less happy proprietor but soon another good owner appears and the life of the people of Gigha grows vigorous once more.

By the time we reach the present day perhaps those of you who know the Island well will view it with new eyes and those of you who still have that pleasure in store will feel, when you arrive in person, that you are welcome to a place you already know well. Above all I hope you all enjoy our exploration into the lives of the people of Gigha.

Part One—The Earliest Times
Chapter 1—Footprints on the sands of time

The first person who is recorded as appreciating the advantages of Gigha is King Haco of Norway who chose its safe Eastern harbours to anchor his Fleet in 1263 as he prepared to fight Alexander III, King of Scotland. Opinion is divided as to whether the Norse called this valuable naval base, which formed the Western bulwark of their extensive naval empire, *Gudey*, meaning God's Island, or whether they regarded it as *Gja-ey* which would signify the Island of creeks where safe harbourage could be enjoyed.[1] Either name would be appropriate. Strategically placed for access to the Mainland or escape to the West, it would indeed be a favourable place to anchor. Curiously enough these two factors have influenced the evolution of the Island over the succeeding centuries.

When the Vikings were refitting their ships for the coming battle they would see much more evidence of former inhabitants of Gigha than you and I can today after many years of cultivation, dyke building and land-reclamation. You and I can find just sufficient evidence to know that people have lived on the Island since three thousand years or so before Christ was born. The footsteps of Stone Age man, Bronze Age and Iron Age folk are just traceable because of their distinctive methods of burying their dead.

We are indeed fortunate in that the distinguished members of the Royal Commission on the Historical and Ancient Monuments of Scotland have recently published the results of their Survey of the Island in *Argyll. Volume 1. Kintyre* which means that we have expert opinion on which of the grassy rock hummocks are Cairns signifying Stone Age burials or Cists of the later Bronze Age or yet Forts or Duns of the Iron Age. So far as I personally am concerned the heather and lichen-covered mounds are part of Gigha's attractive landscape but which is of historical importance and which is not I just wouldn't know.

In writing this book one of the most astonishing features has been that, just when I seemed to be faced with an insoluble problem, help has come from some document or knowledgeable person. In this matter of finding archaeological remains I have been very glad to have the untiring help of a native of Gigha, Betty McNeill, who has spent many years of her free time walking all over the Island identifying sites mentioned by R.S.G. Anderson, that indefatigable archaeologist,[2] and also those seen by the Commissioners. As we shall see she even found a likely Cairn which the Surveyors found, on excavation, was indeed a revealing burial. Even of more value has been her intimate knowledge of the legends and traditions of the Island garnered from her great-uncles and other former inhabitants, lore which would have been lost to us if she had not sought it out and noted what she learnt. However much embroidered over the generations, such handed-down tales very often contain a valuable grain of truth can you but find it which the local historian swallows whole or ignores to his own detriment.

Under Betty's guidance, then, I indulged in my favourite pastime anyway, of walking around on the springy turf and flower-carpetted grass of Gigha. This time I was trying to find the best examples of ancient relics which visitors coming to the Island today can see for themselves. One June morning early in 1978 we set off. The sun shone, a cool breeze blew in our faces, the sea on the East shone aquamarine silver, only lazy waves foamed on the rocks of the rugged West coast. Northwards we went to find *Carn Bhan* where in about 1790 men digging stones for a dyke found a burial place of the Stone Age.[3] The discovery of a large number of ancient stone coffins buried deep underground must indeed have caused a sensation and, not unnaturally, but luckily for us, the minister, the Reverend William Fraser, walked up to the North End to find out what exactly was happening. I say luckily because, as we shall have cause to be grateful for later, the Reverend Fraser was a meticulous man who believed in writing careful accounts of what was happening in his Parish.

On this occasion he recorded " Stone coffins were

discovered by dyke builders — the coffins, of which there were four in the middle of the Cairn, are made up of four large flagstones, forming the bottoms, sides and covers of each with a small flagstone at each end. Two of these coffins are covered, in one of which are human bones. Beside the large coffins are several small coffins, about three feet long, of which only one is entire. On the bottom of one there was a stratum of dark dust about three or four inches deep." Mr. Fraser concluded that a battle had been fought here, but, whether this had been the case or not, he has left us the only eye-witness account of the evacuation of a typical example of a Stone Age Burial in a Communal Cairn on Gigha.

Having reached the North End, away past Kinerarach, Betty struck off the road to the East towards Carn Bhan, "a spread of stones covering a roughly circular area between 17 and 18m in diameter, and standing to a maximum height of one metre." The Kintyre Book goes on to describe the tumbled group which represents four cists, or coffins in the centre while another lies out at the edge. The description ends with an interesting remark: "a considerable quantity of quartz pebbles can be seen in the packing of their immediate vicinity."

We sat in the sunshine munching our apples. The daily steamer, *The Pioneer*, forges ahead towards the Pier, sea-gulls rode the thermals over our heads. Oyster catchers quarrelled noisily down in the Bay.

"Why these quartz pebbles interested me," commented Betty, "is because one day when the Surveyors were here I told them about a stony mound down by Ardlamy Bay which I thought might be a cairn and they actually dug it up on September 17th, 1967. They found the remains of a cist whose cover had gone but inside lay a lot of white stones which they said were part of the ritual of a Stone Age or early Bronze Age burial. I'll show you it someday."[4]

Walking back along the road we passed, near Tarbert Bay the two round humps called the Artisans' Cairns. The legend is that over the narrow isthmus, whose name is derived from *Tar* to drag and *bat* a boat, the men of old used to drag their boats to save going round the North End. We passed carefully the oblong grass-covered hump on the right of the road where a woman was buried. Whether she was an Indian or an Egyptian is a matter of dispute but the fact remains that so strong was the superstition of disturbing her grave that even the hard-headed road makers made a loop around it rather than incur her wrath!

As we went South we talked about these other signs of Stone Age Men, the great stone circles and standing stones, of which so far as we know none has been found on Gigha. At the Druid Stone we halted. Correctly speaking this extraordinary mitten-shaped bit of rock is the *Carraigh an Tarbert*, the Stone of Tarbert. " Funny how fascinated people are with Druids," remarked Betty. " We had two young students here recently who were studying that sort of thing and they said that, if you look

THE DRUID STONE

through the groove you are looking straight at the Northernmost Pap of Jura and that, on Midsummer Day the sun would set right opposite. They said there are stones over on the other side at Ballochroy which is exactly in line and there are other stones in line further on so it was something to do with the sun and astronomy."

We consulted our authority, the Kintyre Book " *Carraigh an Tarbert*, Gigha — a prominent Standing Stone — known as the Druid's Stone — it now leans considerably out of the vertical towards the East and, due to the weathering of a natural fissure, the top is divided into two peaks by a deep indentation." [5]

We laughed together in the sunshine. So far as the *Carraigh an Tarbert* is concerned it seems unlikely to have any connection with the Stone Age. Sometimes I wonder if it was an early signpost marking the place where the North/South Road divided, one section running on down the West of the Island while the other, the present road went along the East coast.[6]

The same mystery, in fact attaches to the other standing stones on Gigha. Up at Keill, Martin Pennant in 1772 discovered a very large stone but he put no date on it and, in any case it has been completely lost.[7] Betty showed me, when we went up there, a curious stile leading into the Achamore Woods which has three large cut stones as steps which are quite different in texture and working from the stones in other stiles as for instance the one opposite it into the Churchyard but whether this is part of Pennant's stone is by no means certain.

The most famous Stone of all is the Ogham Stone, the only one of its kind in the West of Scotland. Common in Southern Ireland, these strange stones with the slanting lines and round markings of Ogham script up one side, Gigha's example is important enough to warrant a whole section of the Kintyre Book to itself.[8] Attempts have been made to decipher the inscription without much success. The Commissioners suggest that possibly the words ' son of Coichele ' can be deciphered but they go on to remark that the stone is probably of the 7th century A.D. so again, although undoubtedly of great interest and antiquity, it is not of the Stone Age.

The fourth standing stone, or rather pair of standing stones are the most mysterious of all, partly because even although they are held, by the people of Gigha, to be very ancient and regarded with awe by some and superstition by others they are entirely ignored by the Commissioners. Standing high on a hillock south of the Lodge the *Bodagh and the Cailleach,* the Old Man and the Old Woman are only a few feet high, one straight, the other shaped like a boat or perhaps a booted foot.[9] Tradition on Gigha is quite clear that, should one or both of them fall it must be re-erected at once or something very unpleasant will happen. Even more curious the Irish, who used to come to Gigha for potatoes as late as to the end of last century treated them with veneration. These are the only stones that nobody has yet put a date to so they might be of great antiquity.

THE   BODACH AND CAILLEACH

In other words the Stone Age Men who buried their dead in communal graves left no reminder of their Stone circles or standing stones on Gigha, which is a pity because from evidence elsewhere it is clear that these megaliths showed a knowledge of astronomical and mathematical appreciation of the seasons and the solar system which show that these people were by no means the savages we sometimes think. In graves in other places evidence has been found which showed that as well as working in stone, they made pottery, wove material and worked wood. So far none of these artefacts has been found on Gigha.

At some time around 2000 B.C. the alloy Bronze was discovered and this sparked off a whole new technology whereby men used the durable metal to make tools, weapons, chariots, articles of adornment, musical instruments and cooking utensils. Of course the further you lived from the centre of civilisation in the Eastern Mediterranean the longer the typical customs and artefacts of the Bronze Age took to reach you, if they arrived at all. Thus it will not surprise you to find that little has been found on Gigha to tell us that Bronze Age Men were there.

Once more our only clue comes from the discovery of some of their graves which are known as Cists and differ from the Stone Age burials in that Bronze Age Men interred their dead in stone coffins in individual graves.[10] Of the nine listed in the Kintyre Book only three are still visible. One is almost hidden under scrub North of Kinerarach, another, in the same overgrown state, lies to the South of North Drumachro. The easiest one for you to see, in fact you can't miss it, lies on a little hill opposite the School.

So far I have followed the experts carefully without suggesting many ideas of my own but, as regards people of the Bronze Age living on Gigha, I have often wondered if perhaps traces of their presence may well lie hidden, overlaid by the progress of centuries. One of the outstanding characteristics of these folk was their habit of making good settlements near a spring surrounded by fertile soil and reasonably good grass. Until only a few years ago each farm on Gigha had its own well and the fertility of the soil is unquestioned. I suppose we'll never know for certain but I think that, where many of Gigha's farms stand today men of the Bronze Age made a settlement. Over the years of recorded history, as we shall discover, with one possible exception, farms have not changed their general location so that although their actual origins are hidden, I feel sure their positions indeed indicate footsteps in the sands of time.

Be that as it may, no doubt exists that by the time of the Iron Age we do find signigicant traces of settlements on the Island. These are in the shape of Forts or Duns, which were settlements defended by a single dry stone or, sometimes turf wall, known on Gigha as a Scraw dyke. The word ' fort ' can be misleading as we tend to equate it with a military fortress, which these lightly defended settlements were not intended to be. Their purpose was mainly to guard the settlement from marauding animals or local robbers. After all such a fortification would be no use at all against a really determined invader as for instance, we shall discover the people of Gigha found in the century when Kintyre was terrorised by the piratical Alan Maclane. Which of the numerous wild animals which roamed the oak forests of Kintyre and the Isles at that time ever reached Gigha we have no means of knowing but, it is clear that the late Bronze Iron Age people of Gigha did build their huts on a small eminence and surrounded the " farm " with either a drystone dyke or a stone and timber wall. The distinction between forts of this kind and duns is often difficult to draw and the distinction made in the Kintyre Book depends almost entirely on internal area-forts being large enough to have served the needs of small communities, while duns are capable of accommodating only a single family group. " Roughly speaking the forts are taken to have exceeded around 4000 square feet while the size of the Duns on Kintyre vary between that and 300 square feet." [11]

Not surprisingly Duns are more common on Gigha than forts, in fact the Kintyre Book lists only one example of a fort which, for some reason is called *Dun Chibhich*[12] which, according to Anderson means Chifie's or Keefie's fort. To find it Betty and I scrambled away up north west of Drumeonbeg Farm to arrive breathless at the top. Keefie, whoever he was, certainly knew how to choose his site! Whether danger threatened by sea or land, he had excellent warning: Islay, Jura, Argyll, Kintyre and all the sea between, most of the East and West expanses of Gigha itself. All these would be within his sights. With a reasonably easily guarded entrance on the East, everywhere else was protected by rocky natural walls. A patch of marshy ground to the West told us where the spring was, although no flag irises grew as they did on the other springs on the Island.

As we slithered down the grass grown slope towards Drumeonbeg I couldn't help wondering if, long after Keefie had gone, some less energetic or less threatened farmer simply shifted his farm down the hill a bit nearer civilisation. The same thought crossed my mind when we went over to the impressive *Dun Trinsse* on the West near Ardailly,[13] which is in a splendid position for defence where a wide area is naturally more or less ringed round by rocks with only one narrow, easily blocked opening towards the sea. Here, for once we could find no spring and thought how much more convenient a site was where nearby Ardailly had been built by the spring.

Before we leave this discussion of forts and duns just let me tell you one other interesting " find " I was shown, by Mr. Bicket, the farmer at Leim, down at the South of the Island. In fact he had some further curious remains to show us later in our story. One day he held out to me a few bits of a hard, blackish rough stoney substance of which he had found quite considerable quantities when ploughing one of his fields. To his surprise he found that similar material was on display in Campbeltown Museum as an example of vitrified stone produced by setting fire to a wall made of stone with a timber framework. The Kintyre Book states that at least one fort elsewhere (Carradale) " is heavily vitrified — which indicates that the original fort may have had a timber framework."[14] Only further excavation will tell us whether Mr. Bicket's queer stone is really significant.

Anyhow, even if you discount the curious features we amateur audacious archaeologists discussed, sufficient evidence exists, properly documented in the Kintyre Book, to tell us that Gigha has been inhabited in turn by men of the Stone Age, who buried their dead communally in cairns, by Bronze Age Men who had cist tombs and began settlements and by Men of the Iron Age who fortified these settlements.

Towards the end of the Iron Age, around 400 A.D. three different groups of people invaded Western Scotland. No mention is made anywhere of Gigha so we can only guess that at least some of these would have visited the Island and influenced its life.

Against the attacks of the first group, the warring sons of Erc, King of Dalriada in Ireland, Keefie's fort and Dun Trinsse would have to be strengthened because these adventurous young men used the Western Isles as a family sparring ground, so much so that it was known as part of Dalriada.

The second band of wanderers would be much more welcome on Gigha. The intinerant Christian missionaries who came from Ireland, led by Columba himself, sailed in their coracles all about the Islands, even penetrating into the Mainland. We, unfortunately, have no hard evidence that any of them came to Gigha but legend tells that St. Cathan, whose headquarters were on Bute, visited the Island of Gigha. Certainly the first church we know about which was built at Keill in the 13th Century, was dedicated to him and there seems no reason at all to doubt that it was he who brought the Christian message to Gigha as well as the knowledge of herbs and crops which the Columban missionaries brought to so many other Islands. [15]

Two relics on Gigha have been suggested as indications of the presence of early missionaries. One is the Celtic Cross in the Field of the Chapel, *Rudh a Chabeil,* near East Tarbert Bay. No doubt exists as to its antiquity but when it was erected on Gigha is not known.[16] The other is the very curious rock discovered in the 30's by Anderson and named by him the Holy Stone which lies among thick undergrowth on the hillside by the Field of the Chapel.[17] Anderson spent a long time trying to decipher the meaning of its peculiar carving. The Kintyre Book simply comments that " it is incised with early Christian symbols " and leaves it at that, which seems to me very wise! [18]

It may be a personal opinion which I base on what I have found in other places, but I regard the traditional Holy Wells as good evidence of very early Christianity being brought by early Christian Missionaries. By Keill road lies the Holy Well of St. Cathan whose waters were considered to cure ailments while the other even more fascinating well is at the edge of East Tarbert Bay. This is the Great Well mentioned by Martin in the 17th Century, which if the appropriate procedure was adopted by a member of the Galbraith family (hence its popular name of the Well of *St. Breathaig)* would forecast the weather for questioning mariners.

The names of these wells may have been altered during the centuries but holy wells where all-important baptisms could be administered are sure signs of very great antiquity.

Whatever the hazy evidence of these two invaders none exists about the third set of people who came from " abroad " to over-run the West of Scotland in the 8th and 9th Centuries, the Norse. Most exciting of all, we at long last can actually see, in the Hunterian Museum in Glasgow University, an exquisite little 10th Century Norse Balance which was dug up last Century on Tarbert Bay by two men making potato pits. Resembling the hand scales of Victorian days, the bronze beam has hinged arms just over eight centimetres long. The indicating needle is Bronze while a decoration of curving lines sets off the little birds which form the suspension links. Opinions differ but it has been suggested that, as the Norse legal system included fines measured in ounces of silver and also other dues, such as marriage dowries, were paid in the same metal perhaps this little balance found on Gigha may have been used to weigh small quantities of silver. The Kintyre Book remarks " it is similar to other such finds in Viking burials elsewhere," a comment which raises the possibility that deep in the sandy soil behind East Tarbert Bay lies a Viking burial. [19]

This of course raises the whole question of the lack of Norse remains on Gigha. We know that the Vikings had conquered all the Western Isles by at latest 900 A.D. many people feel it is strange that only the one relic of all these years of occupation has been found. While it is regrettable I don't think it is very strange. In the first place nobody has so far looked very earnestly in likely sites. To excavate where the Balance was found seems an obvious course of action, or on the hill near Drumachro where tradition holds that Haco stood to review his fleet in Galloichille Bay or perhaps in the marsh behind Ardminish Shore. The answer to that, I suppose, is the expense involved, especially as Gigha is an Island and that much more difficult of access!

Having had my little moan I must confess I am not convinced that many Norse folk lived on Gigha anyway, while burials of Norse heroes may well lie beneath Gigha soil not many of them lived for any length of time on the Island. The facts seem to me to indicate that Gudey was an advanced naval station such as all the maritime powers maintain at strategic points on the fringes of their empires. Maintenance staff may have been stationed there from time to time, around the coast, but otherwise the inhabitants would be left undisturbed.

The people of Gigha by the 13th Century had no reason at all to resent the Norwegians, quite the reverse. Even if, three centuries previously they had been somewhat wild conquerors, they probably were much less troublesome than the Dalriadic princes, especially if all they wanted was safe anchorage, a supply of timber and some local labout for ship-repair. Being Christians by at least the 10th Century, they would not interfere with local religious arrangements, so far as any existed, while their expertise in ship-building and their love of poetry and song would appeal strongly to the men and women who lived on the small Hebridean Island.

Furthermore those same people had no reason at all to feel any loyalty to the King of Scotland, of the Scottish Mainland, quite the reverse. Alexander III himself was the first king who could presume to lay claim to such a title anyway. *Ghamna Gigha* as they were called of old,[20] had ancient ties with Ireland and the Dalriadic Scots, for three centuries they had enjoyed a degree of peace under the Norse. To them this King of Scotland was a foreigner, a landlubber for whom they had no knowledge far less loyalty.

In point of fact the Gigha people may later have looked back on the times of the Norse as happier than living with the incessant strife which broke out among rival clans who each sought to fill the power vacuum left by the departure of the men from Norway, a strife which, far from subduing, the Crown of Scotland used for its own ends. All too often it was itself powerless to stretch out an order-bringing hand to the Hebrides. This general situation was undoubtedly the case but, as we shall see in the next chapter, we have no direct evidence as yet that day-to-day life on Gigha was very much affected by far-off events. To quote Anderson once more " Gigha was too small and too weak to do much else than suffer and endure."[21]

To sum up then; Since about three thousand years before Christ we can trace faint footprints of people living on Gigha, if perhaps intermittently. At the beginning of the Christian era they felt the impact of the fierce Dalriadic Scots and the more civilising influence of the early Christian Missionaries. Sometime during the Ninth Century the Norse conquered the Island along with the rest of the Hebrides and remained for three centuries either as settlers or maintenance men. In 1263 it was these same Norse who first put the Island on the historical map by using it as a naval station before and after the Battle of Largs. When all that has been said we must confess it tells us little about the actual way of life of the people.

Celtic Cross, East Tarbert Bay.

Part Two—The Middle Centuries

The Middle Centuries of Gigha's History, from the departure of the Norsemen in 1266 to the end of the eighteenth Century, might very aptly be called the Dark Ages of Gigha's History.

Away out on the end of the treacherous *Cath Sgeir* rock off the West coast of Gigha a lighted buoy shines out nowadays to guide shipping in the deep waters.[1] At times its ray illuminates brilliantly the surrounding darkness for many miles, at other times the light is blurred by fog while, yet again the fog is patchy so that only sections of sea are clear to the traveller. So it is with our search for knowledge of the life of the inhabitants of Gigha in past days.

From the 13th to the 18th Centuries the fog is very patchy, with only a few faint beams of light to guide us. The late J. MacMaster Campbell put it another way when he remarked " The record is strangely silent about Gigha — strange because of the high strategic value of the Island lying, conveniently, as it does, in the entirely navigable channel between Kintyre and the extensive Island whose coastline so pleasantly interrupts the seascape to the traveller along the western seaboard of Argyll." [2]

This is as true of the Church on Gigha as it is of the effect on the Island of the Clan rivalries during these middle centuries.

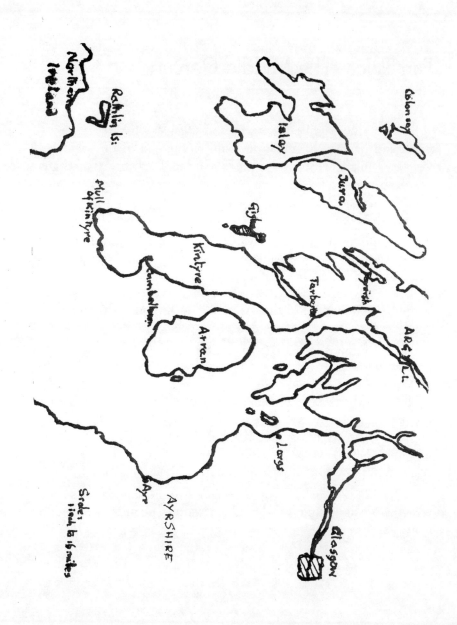

Northern Ireland

Rathlin Is:

Colonsay

Islay

Jura

Gigha

Mull of Kintyre

Kintyre

Campbeltown

Tarbert

Lochgilp...

ARGYLL

Arran

Largs

Ayr

AYRSHIRE

Glasgow

Scale:
1 inch to 16 miles

Chapter 2—The Church

The fog that surrounds the Church life of Gigha between the 13th and 18th Centuries is almost impenetrable; a fact which makes it all the more imperative that we should use to the full the one gleam of illumination we do have. Beside the road to Keill today stands the ruin of St. Cathan's Church which, according to the Kintyre Book " probably dates from the 13th Century." [3] In 1510 James IV presented Angus Makkane to the Rectory of St. Catan, Gigha.[4] In 1549 Dean Munro recorded that on Gigha stood " ane paroche kirke." [5] Over a hundred years later it was visited by Martin.[6] That is the sum total of references to the Church of St. Cathan during the course of some four Centuries.

So we had better stroll up to Keill and look very closely at the old ruin to see what clues we can gather. As we walk up the rough road under the trees of Achamore house we reflect that the dedication to St. Cathan was probably because he was, by the thirteenth Century traditionally associated with the religious life on the Island. A reasonably well documented Columban missionary he had made his Headquarters on Bute from where he travelled far and wide over Kintyre and the Isles in the 6th Century A.D. We have been justified in connecting him with the sacred relics over on West Tarbert Bay and there is no reason to doubt the tradition that he had a cell up here on Keill from where he could look over to Kintyre or gaze westwards over the stormy sea to Islay and his spiritual home in Ireland. A more perfect place for a Columban monk to have a cell I have never seen. He even had a well which is still associated with his name.

That was in the 6th Century. The really crucial question is who the builders were of the 13th Century stone Church that still bears his name? I have no doubt that the men who carried stones up from the beach and mortared them into position were

17

the people of Gigha themselves but whether Gigha possessed an unknown and skilled architect with a knowledge of mainland Kintyre churches or else the Islanders were working to the orders of some person or persons from the mainland, this we'll never know.

Study the stone work and plan of the Church. Forty feet long by some twenty feet wide, the basic plan is an oblong with the short sides facing East and West. On the East end we can still see intact the East window, a long narrow single light window while two smaller single lights lit the Church from the North and South walls opposite each other towards the East end. The door was in the South side, towards the West. The walls, almost three feet thick are " of random rubble laid in lime mortar with window dressings of dark red and coarse-grained yellow sandstone." [7]

Both remaining windows, the East and the one in the North wall have been skillfully built, "deeply splayed " is the phrase used by the Kintyre Book, while the outside has been " chamfered." If you look carefully you'll find a small Latin cross carved on the inside of the wall on the North side and, outside on another carefully dressed stone, a Greek Cross.

Look back again at the description of the stones which form the Church, the " random rubble " looks to me as though some of it at least could have been obtained on Gigha but the dark red and coarse-grained sandstone must have been brought to the Island from somewhere else.

Anderson suggests that the MacDonalds built it as " they owned Gigha in these times." [8] Apart from the fact that he does not specify exactly what " these times " were I doubt if the state of the Western Isles after the Norse departure was conducive to any clan having time or money or indeed inclination to build such a Church. In my opinion it is more likely that the monks of the Cistercian Abbey at Saddell on Kintyre at least organised the erection of the Church either for the sole use of the inhabitants or partly as a place of retreat for themselves. They dedicated the Church to the traditional Gigha Saint while his Holy Well was used, as perhaps he had used it, for Baptisms and healings.

I doubt if we shall ever know the exact truth about the building of the Church, mainly because hardly any documents about the Cistercian Abbey at Saddell have survived. In 1507 James IV declared that there had been no monastic life there in living memory and he transferred its assets, such as they were, to the Bishopric of Argyll who promptly built a castle with them.[9] A couple of years later the same king granted to Saddell two Merklands on Gigha "of the lands of Cragvan."[10] Such as the thirteenth Century monks possessed may be reposing deep in the archives of the Vatican or in some ecclesiastical cellar but so far they have not been found.

Of the Font seen by Martin on the Altar[11] in the 17th Century the Kintyre Book remarks "It is not possible to ascribe this font to any particular date within the medieval period."[12] The reason for its being on the Altar when Martin saw it is not clear but this may have been due to some disturbance connected with the Reformation. Happily' it has now been restored to its proper resting place in the present Parish Church of Gigha.

Kilchattan Church

The numerous great stone burial slabs both inside and outside the Church have excited the interest of various authorities. T. P. White writing in the 1870's recorded ten of the decorated slabs, each some six feet long by three feet wide, tapered, as might be expected like a coffin.[13] Anderson describes nine[14] while the latest survey by the Kintyre Book Archaeologists records that they found seven only.[15]

Many of them are very worn and the design difficult to decipher. One of the best has as its central feature a sword surrounded by many whorls and feathery scrolls. What fascinates me about this particular stone is the plain rectangle above the sword where someone, long ago, had carved a comb, a pair of shears, a weird figure, which the Kintyre Book notes depicts a " Mermaid," and a thin pointed implement. Among the scroll work you can just trace a couple of animals identified as an otter and salmon, which appear to be chasing each other in and out of the foliage.

As all are carved in local stone it seems to me that, so far as our present intention of trying to reconstruct what Gigha people did in the Middle Ages, these magnificent stones bear witness to the artistic bent and carving expertise of long dead Gigha masons. No name was considered necessary to identify a tombstone, his signs alone told parishioners who was buried where. It is unfortunate that we have lost the key to the carvings.

The strangest slab of all lies away over, outside the Church, to the East. To see it you may have to crawl about and pull away the grass when, there outlined on the slab, stands a determined looking middle aged warrior complete with " kilt " and sword. Anderson found this stone and photographed it.[16] To the Islanders this is known as " Malcolm's grave " and the tradition is that it marks the grave of Malcolm McNeill who died in 1493. I find this to be very curious. Why one out of the many McNeill's connected with the Island should be so universally remembered in connection with this stone it is difficult to see, except it is in fact the truth which has been passed down, in which case I feel Malcolm McNeill must have been a well known and respected figure on the Island.

Before we leave the Church notice a few more modern tombstones among the old graves. Near the North wall of the Church stand three stones, one is too worn to make out what it once held, another is in memory of "James Stevenson of Ardlammie who died the 1st of August 1858." The third is decorated with a coat of arms which Anderson remarks is the Stevenson insignia.[17] It is simply carved "James Stephenson Ardglammy." Remember these stones when we come to discussing Ardlammy.

The final stone **which** is of significance to us in the present search I myself have never actually managed to see properly. Near Malcolm's grave is a stone very much overgrown. This is, I believe the tomb of Neil Simpson who was the first minister of the Parish of Gigha and Cara. [18]

In pre-Reformation days we noted the appointment "by royal authority of Angus Makkane in succession to Sir John Judge" so it seems probable that, at that time Gigha had a priest of its own. From 1626 to 1641 Gigha appears to have been joined to Colonsay and Jura.[19] In 1641 the minister from Saddell was "to repair to Gigha every six weeks." This does not seem to have been satisfactory and in 1642 Gigha was joined to Killean. By that time Scotland was once more in a state of turmoil and, as had happened before, in the chaos Gigha was forgotten so that in 1654 the Synod of Argyll said that Gigha was desolate because no minister visited the Island.

The Synod's answer to this was to re-join Gigha to Killean but, not for the last time their reverences were to find the people of the small Island capable of standing up for their rights. They did it quite simply by sending no tithes over to Kintyre and even more effectively by omitting to send a boat over to fetch a minister. They wanted a resident minister of their own.

Still against a background of national upheaval resulting from the defection of James II in 1688 and the arrival of William of Orange, further complicated by the War against France over the Spanish succession, it is no wonder that chaos prevailed in Church matters as regards Gigha. On one occasion the Killean minister decamped with all the Church records (again this was not the last time this happened to Gigha) and on another the minister in charge was deposed by the Presbytery for drunkenness and profanity. Then another attempt was made to join Gigha to Jura and Colonsay and this time Jura and Colonsay refused the deal.

Here I wonder what happened, or who came to Gigha in or about 1707 because in that year someone took the matter in hand and a new church was built at Ardminish, just opposite the present hotel.[20] Not only that but the school was built at the same time although I do not know exactly where. Finally in 1717 Gigha and Cara were declared to be a separate parish and a minister called Neil Simpson was appointed in charge of the new Parish.

In 1761 it was decided to design a new glebe " because the town of Keill was church lands and there was still ruins of a church and manse." Remember that manse, it may be very important later. By this time Neil Simpson was dead and his successor, William Mowat complained that the Church at Ardminish had fallen into ruin. Finally in 1780 a " new " church was built on the site of the old one at Ardminish which remained the parish church of Gigha and Cara till the present Church was built in 1923.

You will have noticed that I remarked in passing that I feel somebody of importance arrived on Gigha around 1707. One reason for my saying this was that, at the later date of 1780, another new Laird came to Gigha and began a new era in the Island's history and I feel it was more than coincidence that at the same time Gigha not only had a new church but also, a few years later a new school and an efficient minister, so perhaps the same had happened earlier.

In modern times the character of the proprietor has been all important to the Island so I think it's time we retraced our steps to see what we can learn about those who held the Island in the past, when the Western Isles were rent with the bitter rivalry between the clans to fill the power vacuum left by the departure of the Norsemen.

Chapter 3—Rivalry between the clans

After the Treaty of Perth in 1266 the Western Isles including Gigha undoubtedly belonged to the King of Scotland, at that time Alexander III.[1] Obviously he had to appoint a lieutenant to rule and guard the Western approaches to Scotland. Equally he had to reward the warriors who had helped him defeat the Norse. Therefore one would feel that a person deserving of the King's trust would be John of the Isles, he whose original desertion of Haco played a crucial part in the final downfall of the Norwegian power.

This may have happened but we just do not have any charter that proves it. The Kings of Scotland during the rest of the thirteenth Century were much too busy trying to preserve their own independence from the English to pay much attention to the Isles. Whether such a deed ever existed or not I doubt if we'll ever know because, in the desperate struggle against the English during the later part of the 13th Century, it is not surprising that many state papers were either never executed or have been lost.

On the other hand there is little doubt that John of the Isles' successors remained high in the Royal favour. Apart from the grant, in 1309 by Robert I to the Earl of Mar of lands in Kintyre, including the *Island of Gug,* the first legal document we have after the Kings of Scotland had consolidated their position, is a document dated 1343. By this David II granted extensive lands, including the *Island of Githey* to John, Lord of the Isles, Chief of the MacDonalds of the Isles.

For a Century the McDonalds remained Lords of the Isles until in 1493 the Crown took the title into its own care. The 16th Century was possibly the most troubled in all Scottish History, a state of affairs which rendered the Crown almost powerless to curb the vicious struggle between the three clans of

McDonald, McLain and Campbell for power over Argyll and the Western Isles. MacMaster Campbell sums up the History of this Century: " a confused time, with many transmissions and cross-transmissions of land."[2]

As the 16th Century went on it gradually became clear that the Campbells under their chiefs, the Earls of Argyll, were in the ascendant. Their loyalty to the Crown, to which they were related by marriage, was unswerving as was their devotion to the Protestant Church. After 1631 when John McDonald surrendered his lands in Kintyre to Archibald, the 7th Earl of Argyll and Marquis of Lorne and Kintyre, the Campbells were undisputed holders of Argyll under the King of Scotland.

As time went on feudal rights and obligations became obsolete and the final tie with the past, so far as Gigha was concerned, was broken in 1976 when the last vestige of the old system vanished when the feu duty was redeemed by the payment of £224.07.[3]

This brings us back to Gigha. What was happening to the little Island in its " vitally strategic position " while the great ones were locked in this power struggle? For the succinct answer I turn again to Anderson. " Gigha, lying on the edge of two fairways must have felt the eddies of the currents that swept the Sounds and Channels. Through it all Gigha was too small and too weak to do much else but suffer and endure."[4] That Gigha survived the troubled times was mainly due to the far-sighted policy of the Clan McNeill of Taynish to which the Island was entrusted by successive Lords of the Isles.

When, back in the fifteenth Century John McDonald had been given the Lordship of the Isles, he, like the king himself, had shared his power out among his supporters and he chose those whom he thought would best guard his territory. To Torquil McNeill of Taynish he entrusted the Constableship of the important Castle Sweyn together with lands in Kintyre, which included Gigha; this gave him the title of Tosheodire of Kintyre. Torquil was in effect third step down in feudal hierarchy; he held Gigha of McDonald who in turn held it of the King of Scotland.

So much then for what we might call the outer layer of Gigha's history throughout the middle centuries. A closer examination of some of the deeds will give us a faint glimpse of the Island itself. Fortunately for us McDonald's original grant to Torquil McNeill did not include the whole of Gigha. Who held other parts we do not know but they were probably, as was the custom, members of the McDonald clan itself.

Be that as it may, Torquil had authorty in Gigha over one eighth of Arydalch (Ardailly), one eighth of Arydagh (Ardachy), two eighths of Drumyhaynvoir, (Drumeonmore), an eighth of Aryduirmegynche (Ardminish), one eighth of Arydgkannich (Ardlammy) and one eighth of Fairyfown. Where this last was I haven't discovered. The name disappears by the next Century so it must have become merged with another clachan. The only clue I can suggest is that *Carn na Faire* is named by Anderson as being a Watch Cairn at the North End so perhaps Fairyfown is now part of Kinerarach. This is the first list I have found of the actual names of places on Gigha. Each holding was described as so many " merklands " the old Scots measurement of land, and the explanation of the division of holdings is that each named place was a communal farm or clachan, a point which will become abundantly clear later.

At the moment it seems strange that the possession of eighths of clachans on Gigha was of any very great importance, but subsequent history shows that even these seemingly tiny fractions gave the McNeills of Taynish a firm foothold on the Island. During the rest of the sixteenth Century succeeding Lords of the Isles confirmed the grant to succeeding McNeills of Taynish. The McNeills behaved with such perspicacity, that, even when as we have seen James IV invested the title of Lord of the Isles in the Crown in 1493, not only do we find they retained the various eighths in a charter from James V in 1531 but in 1542 Neil McNeill (possibly grandson or maybe great grandson of the original Torquil) was granted by the King the " £20 lands of Gigha," in other words the entire Island which consisted of the following: Cannerraroch, Tarbert, Ardalay, Ardachy, Ardeglammes, Chantereoch (probably later Achamore), Layme, Kilchattan, Ardewiginis (Ardminish), Drumguonmoir, Drumguonbeg, Saul

25

and Drumcro. Fairyfown we've noticed has over the centuries been absorbed by somewhere else, and in later documents Saule becomes Scoull and then Scoull of Drumcro in deeds which include another Drumchro, so I think it must be the old name for one of the Drumachro farms, possibly South Drumachro.

My reason for considering that the McNeills were wise in their generation is not only that they successfully weathered the storms of the fifteenth Century under the McDonalds but were still in Gigha when the Campbell influence began to prevail in the 16th Century. As early as 1519 Neil McNeill of Gaeya was a friend and servitor of Colin, 3rd Earl of Argyll so their political judgement of who was likely to win the overlordship eventually was accurate and they acted accordingly.

They survived even the tragic incident in 1530 when Allan McLean, a "reckless and ambitious spirit, with conspicious genius for direct action, took the sea as a pirate." "Allan-na-Sop" as he was nicknamed, roamed the Western seas, killing and plundering indiscriminately and in 1530 he landed on Gigha, murdered Neil McNeill and many of the inhabitants of Gigha and destroyed much of their property. In spite of this James V legalised Neil McNeill, son of the murdered McNeill, in the £20 lands of Gigha which was by then named a Barony, which in Scotland denoted a large manor held of an overlord.

After the death of James V in 1542 and the succession of the child Mary, Queen of Scots, the weakness of the Crown led to the confusion which MacMaster Campbell calls "kaleidoscopic changes in the feudal ownership of Gigha, some of them inconsistent with the grant immediately prededing." Then Dean Munro wrote, in 1549, that "the auld thane of Gigay should be Laird of the same, call it McNeill of Gigay and now it is possessed by Clan Ranald" (the McDonalds). [5]

I agree it was indeed a confused time generally but this is where I particularly wish we could locate the McNeill Charters to find out if part of the apparent confusion over possession of Gigha resulted from the habit of dividing up the Island between different people, a custom which we shall find, persisted until 1865, when for the first time since at least the 17th Century, the

Island was united under one Laird. The grants in the 16th Century may very well have been contradictory but I cannot help wondering if each one referred to different eighths or whatever of the Island. True, each grant may have *begun* by referring to the " £20 lands of Gigha " but later Charters which began with that statement, in the small print so to speak, went on to mention certain exceptions which were to belong to someone else.

The truth was that the McNeills themselves repeated the process of granting parts of the Island to their own cadet or younger branches, most notably in 1673 when Roger McNeill granted to Donald McNeill of Galdchailzie (our modern Galloichille) on Loch Sweyn " my kinsman, 2 merklands of Luime, 2 merklands of Drumyeonbeg, 1 merkland of Drinto or Drumchro and the Isle of Gigulum." [6] This Charter incidentally is the earliest legible document preserved among the estate papers in Edinburgh. Sheriff MacMaster Campbell refers to this with reference to the reaction on Gigha to the landing of William of Orange in 1689. " Some jibbed at the Dutchman," he said " including McNeill of Galloichille, a cadet of the McNeills of Taynish who with McDonald of Largie and McLean of Duart raised a small sept for King James." McNeill of Gigha, on the other hand, prudently remained faithful to the Duke of Argyll in supporting the Protestant King. Galloichille is not recorded as having done anything. McNeill of Gigha made a foray to Islay but " returned quietly to Gigha." [7]

Regarding the '45 MacMaster Campbell remarked that " McNeill of Gigha remained loyal to the Government." [8] This is not surprising as his overlord was the Duke of Argyll and we have already seen that the McNeills were not given to rash behaviour! To me the real puzzle is who is meant by " McNeill of Gigha "? Nowhere is it suggested nor is it in the least likely that McNeill of Taynish was known as McNeill of Gigha. Probably this mysterious man was another younger branch of the Taynish family but for almost the whole 18th Century the historical black-out is complete.

Only one brilliant ray of light stabs the darkness lightening for an instant one facet of life on the Island. The same beam will shed light on much of our researches into the 19th Century. Let me tell you about it!

Interlude—Brief bright encounter

On a clear sunny day last June (1978) I was walking over to the Mill of Ardailly with Mr. and Mrs. McNeill Kivett whom I had met by chance in the Shop. They had travelled to Gigha all the way from North Carolina to see where Mr. McNeill Kivett's ancestors had been the millers of ·Gigha in the late seventeenth and early eighteenth centuries.

Their story shed a brilliantly illuminating ray of light, not only into that foggy period of Gigha History but, in the afterglow, so to speak, I could dimly perceive developments which might explain much of the early nineteenth century on the Island. The whole romantic episode belongs both to the past and the present. Come with us and listen!

We trekked over the spine of Gigha, across the road which leads to Ardailly from Drumeonmore Farm. The road was rough with the stones brought over by generations of Gigha farmers in their carts for their meal, carts full of the stones which were required as part payment for having their grain ground. At last we came to the old stone mill, whose fourteen foot walls are still standing. The mill enclosed an area of thirty-six feet by twenty-two while the grain store measured twenty-three feet by eighteen. The huge iron Mill wheel which was placed there last century by the grandfather of the present tenant of the Croft, Mr. Hugh Wotherspoon, still hangs in its place.

As the three of us sat looking out over the wide expanse of sea beyond the Mill, Mr. McNeill Kivett told me about Neil and Grisella McNeill, the very earliest inhabitants of Gigha about whom we know many personal details. Away back in the seventeenth century the Mill of Ardailly on Gigha was worked by one Hector McNeill who came from Islay. In due course Hector's son Neil succeeded to his father's two merklands of Ardailly but bought another two so that by about 1727 he had a reasonably valuable holding. Neil had married a lady called Grisella and, whether it was Neil or Grisella or both of them who were ambitious we don't know, but in 1738 they sold the Mill to one John McLachlan and set sail, with their family for America.

There they landed in North Carolina, between South Carolina and Virginia. In North Carolina lived other Scottish settlers encouraged thither by a Scottish Governor called Gabriel Johnson who was offering plots freehold, fifty acres of land to anyone who cared to come from Scotland. To those who, like Neil and Grisella had sons it was not difficult to amass a sizeable estate and become much richer and more important than they ever would have been as tenants on Gigha. Among their children was a daughter called Nigelina and it is from her, some nine generations on that Mr. McNeil Kivett is descended. It is all detailed in his Family Bible.

Not only is this a romantic true story but it is also a very revealing one. Mr. Kivett told me that letters do exist (though not to Neil and Grisella) from people in North Carolina to friends in Scotland encouraging them to emigrate. In fact in America definite evidence exists of a publicity campaign for emigrants.

The three of us sat in silence, gazing out towards the Paps of Jura each thinking of that ship on which Neil and Grisella set out adventuring all these years ago. My mind returned to life on Gigha itself. It seems highly unlikely that Neil and Grisella sailed alone with their family. Almost certainly other friends from the Island, lured by the thought of free-hold land where, by their own efforts they could become prosperous, went with them. After all sailing across stormy waters held few terrors for them.

As though reading my mind Mrs. McNeill said, thoughtfully " It would seem quite natural for them just to sail. After all America was just a bit further on than Islay or Jura."

That afternoon's conversation at Ardailly lay at the back of my mind when I returned home to study the nineteenth Century and I found that the implications of these two early McNeills setting out may very well underlie much of the evolution of Gigha during that century.

Part 3—Modern Times (since about 1780)

To resume our story: by the end of the Eighteenth Century a new era was about to begin in the history of Gigha. Within the last twenty years of that century Gigha acquired a new Proprietor in John McNeill who was the first of an almost unbroken line of resident lairds who took a deep personal interest in the good of the Island. Then, too, a new Minister was appointed who not only was a zealous pastor but left valuable records of his pastorate. The re-building of the Church in 1780 and the development of the new school which was erected about 1790 widened further the cultural horizons of the Island. With the help of the ever increasing volume of records we can trace the changes in the life of the inhabitants during the nineteenth and early twentieth Centuries.

On the whole, though, life on Gigha did not change as spectacularly as life did on the Mainland. The air was still clean and fresh, the translucent sea beckoned profitably to the Fishermen, the fertile soil rewarded the Farmers. But change it did. Tenant farmers cultivated the fields more profitably than had been possible under the old clachan system and, although most people were wage-earning, incomes were more certain. As the nineteenth century progressed many of the old black houses were replaced by more comfortable cottages.

The potential of the Island increased, very gradually, as things do in the Islands. In time, steam ships and larger sailing ships ploughed up and down Gigha Sound taking produce to ever-widening markets and providing ready means of communication with the outside world. Produce, stock and, above all, people could travel relatively easily to and from Gigha.

OFF TO THE FIELDS. *Scene of Old Scottish Country Life. By kind permission of the artist, Edna Whyte from Old Rectory Designs, Island of Luing, Argyll.*

Old Pioneer

Chapter 4—Modern proprietors

Whatever may have happened in previous centuries the personalities and policies of the various owners of the Island since the late 18th Century have had a profound effect on life on Gigha. The next logical subject to consider therefore is that of the modern lairds of Gigha.

Most of us think of Gigha as one Estate, belonging to a single person, but, in fact this has been true only since 1865. The Reverend William Fraser wrote in 1791 that *"five-sixths* of Gigha belonged to Mr. McNeill of Gigha and the remaining *sixth* to Mr. McNeill of Galloichoille."[1] A close study of the considerable body of Estate papers amplifies this statement. The five-sixths belonging to Mr. McNeill of Gigha comprised the Island as we know it today with the notable exception of the farms of Leim, North Drumachro and Drumeonbeg and the Island of Gigulum. This, the remaining sixth mentioned by Mr. Fraser was, at least from the end of the eighteenth Century till 1865 in the possession of a cadet branch of the McNeill's – the McNeill's of Galloichille on Loch Sweyn from whom the small property took the name Galloichille. This division of the Island can be followed in detail till 1865 when J. Williams Scarlett of Thryberg in Yorkshire bought both estates in separate deals, thus uniting the Island under one proprietor, as it has remained ever since.

I suggest we follow the history of the ownership of the two Estates separately, taking the Main Estate first.

At last we have some hard evidence. We know who the first proprietor was and we know exactly what Mr. Fraser meant by the five-sixths and the one-sixth into which the Island was divided. The first resident owner of Gigha, so far as we know, was John McNeill of Colonsay. What exactly lay behind the negotiations is not clear. Possibly McNeill of Taynish was short of money but, for some reason, secured permission from the Duke of Argyll, the Overlord of the Island, to sell it to John McNeill who was probably a relation.

Authorities differ about the actual date of the transaction. Anderson puts it at 1780[2] while Mr. Fraser, the contemporary Minister of the Parish wrote that " Mr. McNeill came in 1788." [3] Be this as it may, in the Estate Papers in Edinburgh the first Sasine, the document which legalised his possession of Gigha, is dated 1797. In this handwritten document the Duke grants to " John McNeill his heirs and assignees whatsoever heritabley and irremediably all and whole those parts and portions of the lands and barony of Gigha viz: Careronit, Tarbert, Ardaly, Ardelamy, Chancereoch, Kilchattan, Ardevagnies, Drumyeonmore, Scoul, and Dunchro with the Manor place, home, biggings gardens, Tofts, Crofts, Milnes, Multures and sequels thereof. Woods fishings as well in salt water as in fresh water annexes, connexes, dependancies and all and sundry parts, pendicles and pertinents thereof lying within the Sheriffdom of Argyll with the Office of Baillie and Officiary or Serjeantry within the haill bounds of the lands and barony of Gigha so far as the said offices can now be exercised and are not abolished by an Act of 1743 abolishing heritable jurisdictions in Scotland. – But always excepting out of the same charter the lands of Luime, Drumyeonbeg, Duncro and other parts of the said lands and barony of Gigha feued by Roger Hamilton McNeill of Taynish and his predecessors and another to Daniel McNeill of Galloichille and his predecessors."

John McNeill therefore owned our modern Kinerarach, Tarbert, Ardailly, Ardlamy, Chancereoch (Achamore), Ardminish, Drumeonmore, Scoul (now part of South Drumachro), Kilchattan, and South Drumachro. His property included such Mills as the Island possessed, woods and all fishings as well as other outlying parts. But he did not own Leim, Drumeonbeg, North Drumachro or the Isle of Gigulum which were still feued by Taynish and held by Daniel McNeill of Galloichille.

While it is not stated in this Sasine, subsequent documents show that two of the farms, Ardlammy and Ardailly were held by John McNeill under special feuedal terms. At Ardlammy a family called Stevenston lived, as we saw when we were looking at the tombstones in the grave-yard. Robert Stevenson died in 1798 leaving his farm to his son, Colin. The deed recording this goes on to say that " Robert Stevenson owed John McNeill the sum of £83 12s. 4d. Finally, in 1799 John bought the whole farm for £1936 since when it has been an integral part of the Main Estate.

Neil and Grisella's old home at Ardailly poses an odd problem. In 1769 John McNeill bought Neil's old four merklands from John MacLachlan's son Donald for 12,000 marks Scots. This gave John control of the four merklands at Ardailly together with " houses, biggings yeards with the two corn mills built upon the said lands of Ardailly – grazings – ships belonging to the two mills – together with the water going to and from the Dam to the said mills with the liberty of quarrying quern stones wherever they can be found." This all, you will notice was before he officially came to the Island so he must have had a considerable interest even before Anderson's date of 1780.

Incidentally the Miller would not need to go far for the said quern stones as you can still see from where he quarried them from a rock below Ardlammy. Not that I believe for a minute that all the querns quarried reached the Mill. Several querns, some of them unbroken lie on farms and gardens all over the Island or are built into walls.

To return to the Mill. John's possession of it was ratified by the 1787 Sasine and, from then on, the Miller was a tenant of the Laird. Probably the Mill Croft, which still exists, dates from this time when the Miller ceased to own the land but was allowed a certain amount for his own use. When we come to read the late 18th Century Session Records we shall find that Malcolm Blue and then his son Donald were the millers.

As to the Mill lochs, I have been told that one is natural while the others are artificial. Donald MacDonald, who is today the oldest man on the Island tells me that his grandfather was " at the digging " of the artificial ones which would bring that event to the beginning of the 19th Century.

When that century opened John McNeill was busy improving the viability of his property and the lives of his tenants, as we shall see in detail in our next chapter. In 1818 John died to be succeeded by his son, another John who was granted the Estate in exactly the same words as his father had been; all Gigha with the exception of Leim, Drumachro, Drumeonbeg and Gigulum.

We can only guess at the activities of this John McNeill. All we know is that they were not confined to the Island of Gigha. He may or may not have been a good landlord, this we don't know. What we do know is that he mortgaged Gigha for £8,000 and, when he was declared bankrupt on June 21st, 1832, Gigha had to be sold to help pay his debts which amounted to the fantastic sum of £66,889 14s. 5½d. As his total assets amounted to £39,263 1s. 1½d. he was declared bankrupt.

It is probable that John McNeill was heavily involved in one of the many private banks which failed all over England and Scotland at this time. In John's case the Bank concerned may have been the Renfrewshire Banking Company, Greenock. The complainants who actually brought the case against him were two ministers, the Reverend J. and the Reverend John Yorstoun and their sister Miss Anna Yorstoun. The relevant Estate Document contains several foolscap pages naming his creditors, most of whom belong to professional classes, doctors, ministers, lawyers and several charitable societies.

Curiously enough the interesting point for us lies not so much in how he had managed to amass such a huge debt but in the valuations of the Island on behalf of the creditors. One of the bulkiest documents in the black tin box of Estate papers is Document 31 which, dated 1832, is " An abstract of the prepared sale of lands in Gigha – A forced sale brought on by the bankruptcy of John McNeill." Then follows a detailed survey of all the farms and cottages on Gigha, with, of course the notable exception of Leim, Drumeonbeg, Drumachro and Gigulum. Each valuer listed his estimation of the estimated value of the farms and cottages together with a record of the actual rent each paid and then each added his own comments on the state of the Island, usually with advice as to how it could be improved.

At this distance of time little of value is gained by detailing actual money values, apart from anything else money at the end of 18th century for land was very variable anyway. Of real interest to us is the fact that Ardlamy was by far the most valuable farm with Achamore and Kinerarach. Tarbert was not far behind. Remember of course we are minus a Drumachro, Drumeonbeg and Leim. Even though if we glance into the future we find that when we have a list of value of farms in 1911 this is almost exactly the case; as indeed it is throughout all the valuations of the 19th Century!

We'll be noting later how much money people earned so perhaps it's worth recording that for the four cottages at New Quay each tenant paid £3, a sum that varied little for over a hundred years. Of the four at Keill three cost £3 each a week and one, the dearest on the Island, fetched a rent of £5. The cottages at Ardminish too paid this £3 rent with one at £5.

We find names we shall meet again like Galbraith and McDonald, McNeill, Smith, McCougan, Graham, Henderson and McQuilken, names we can still find on Gigha today. One man I feel sure must have been especially prosperous: Malcolm McKellar who was the tenant not only of Ardlammy and half Carnvickoie but was also in charge of Achamore.

The Surveyors were unanimous that progress would not be made until leases of more than one year were granted by the proprietor. Another cause of lack of revenue was that "neither tenants nor cottars consider that they are bound to pay in money or service when not required" and Mr. McNeill exacted nothing in lieu of services such as road-making or harvest. They were also unanimous that some money ought to be spent on "blasting of rocks and draining and sub-dividing of land."

The total value of Gigha was calculated to be £39,263 6s 6d., which included various estimates of the purchase of the various rentals. Setting this against the total, including interest, of Mr McNeill's debts he was, not surprisingly, declared bankrupt.

What happened to John McNeill himself is not known but fortunately disaster for Gigha was averted by the action of one John Carstairs who, in 1836 bought the Island. John's daughter

Elizabeth was the wife of John McNeill's son Alexander. John Carstairs declared, " I have, for the love, favour and affection I have and bear to Alexander McNeill, son of John McNeill Esq., of Colonsay and Gigha and Elizabeth Carstairs, his spouse, my own fourth daughter – buy this purchase in life rent to myself – and then – to Alexander McNeill and his spouse Elizabeth Carstairs – and their heirs."

When John Carstairs bought Gigha Alexander McNeill and his wife Elizabeth had three boys, John Carstairs McNeill, Alexander and Duncan. More children must have been born to them because in 1850 Alexander and three of his sons were drowned off the coast of Wigtownshire. Their bodies must have been brought to Gigha as their wall tombstone stands in Kilchattan Churchyard today.

When his father died, his son John Carstairs McNeill heired the Estate but by that time he had become a Captain of the Royal Native Infantry in Auckland, New Zealand, so he appointed an Alexander McNeill, W.S. Edinburgh to act for him in the matter of his estate. No mention is made of this Alexander being a relation.

In 1865 John Carstairs McNeill authorised the sale of the Island to one James Williams Scarlett of Thrybergh Park, Yorkshire who " for that part of the Island belonging to John Carstairs McNeill paid the sum of £38,200." So Gigha came into the possession of a new family, a family whose next three representatives were to take Gigha still further along the road of progress.

There, for the moment we must leave the Main Estate to return to the history of that part of Gigha which Roger McNeill of Taynish had granted in 1673 to his kinsman Donald of Galdchailzie on Loch Sweyn. We have seen that the Largie papers record that in 1689 the owner, still a Mr. McNeill, was inclined to support King James II but he was not noted as doing anything to help the King's cause.

At first I had a suspicion that the named 2 merklands of Luime, 2 merklands of Drumeonbeg, 1 merkland of Drumcro and the Islet of Gigulum might refer to *parts* of these farms only, but such doubts were dispelled by the explicit exception of the farms as a whole from the Sasines on 1797 and 1818 and their complete absence from the valuations and the subsequent sale of the estate in 1836 to John Carstairs.

We find further conclusive evidence of this in the contemporary reports by two separate ministers. In 1791, as we have seen, the Reverend Fraser stated " five sixths of the land belongs to Mr. McNeill of Gigha with the remaining sixth to Mr. McNeill of Galloichille." Over fifty years later the then incumbent, the Reverend James Curdie wrote " the landowners of the Parish are Captain Alexander McNeill, younger of Colonsay and the Lady of the Hon. A. H. Morton and Miss MacDonald Lockhart, daughter of the late Sir Charles MacDonald Lockhart, of Lee and Carnwath. The Parish is divided into thirty-one merklands of which Cara forms one, twenty-five belong to Captain McNeill and the remaining six to the Lady of the Hon. A. H. Morton and Miss MacDonald." [4] [1]

The gap then, in our knowledge of the Galloichille estate is between the accounts of the two Ministers. Mr. Fraser in 1791 recorded that it belonged to Mr. McNeill while, by the time Mr. Curdie wrote, Mrs. Moreton MacDonald and her sister Miss MacDonald were the owners. We therefore must trace the changes of ownership between 1791 and 1845.

In 1789 Dr. James McNeill was granted the estate by Roger Hamilton McNeill of Taynish and he, in turn, handed it over to Daniel McNeill, " great-grandson and nearest male heir of Donald McNeill." In the next Sasine, dated 1803, the holder was named as " Henry Frederick McNeill nearest male heir and brother-german to Daniel McNeill." By 1834 Henry Frederick had died and was succeeded by " his heir " Malcolm McNeill. Whether Malcolm ever lived on Gigha seems doubtful because his business was conducted by one Charles Ferrier, the Factor of the Largie estate. One thing certain about Malcolm is that he had no male heir.

That much was easy to trace as it is all in the estate papers and the Register of Sasines. The next clear deed dated 1839 records that, in that year, Charles Ferrier, on behalf of

Malcolm McNeill granted Leim, Drumeonbeg, Drumcro and Gigulum to two sisters, Miss Mary Jane MacDonald Lockhart and her sister Miss Emilia Olivia MacDonald Lockhart of Lee and Carnwath in Lanarkshire. I had almost despaired of finding out why these ladies were heirs of Galloichille in Gigha, when I had one of these lucky breaks which so often have come when I am almost giving up.

It so happens that I myself spent much of my childhood after we left Gigha on the Lee and Carnwath Estate so I contacted Mr. Simon MacDonald Lockhart, the present Laird of the ancient property. By invitation I visited him at his house near Carnwath where, sitting under portraits of past Lairds of Lee and Carnwath, he showed me his family tree where I discovered the answer to my problem of the little estate away over on Gigha.

On 29th March 1798 Jane McNeill of Galloichille married, in Gigha, Alexander MacDonald sixteenth Laird of Largie, twenty-first Laird of Lee and sixth Laird of Carnwath which was indeed a brilliant marriage.[5] In due course their eldest son Charles, inherited these various ancient properties as well as also being his mother's heir so that on the death of Malcolm McNeill of Galloichille, as Charles MacDonald Lockhart had also died, the heirs to Galloichille were declared to be his daughters, jointly, Mary Jane and Emilia Olivia, who incidentally was named after her mother, Charles Lockhart's wife. In 1837 Mary Jane married the Hon. Augustus Moreton and so became " the Lady of the Hon. Augustus Moreton." What this comes to is that Malcolm McNeill's inheritance of three farms and an Islet on Gigha passed, to the Lockhart sisters through the marriage of Jane McNeill of Galloichille in Gigha to their grand-father.

In 1849 Mary Jane and Emilia Olivia divided Galloichille between them: Emilia had the lands of Drumeonbeg and " the six crofts adjoining " (the first time we find documentary proof that these belonged to the smaller estate), while Mary Jane had Leim, one croft at Drumeonbeg " (the South most)," the Ferry, the Glebe and the Island of Gigulum.

Sadly, both these ladies died childless within a year of each other, Emilia Olivia in 1850 and Mary Jane in 1851. This meant that their inheritance reverted to their widowed mother

Dame Emilia Olivia who in 1865 sold the Galloichille estate to J. Williams Scarlett for the sum of £10,800. The transaction together with J. Williams Scarlett's purchase of the rest of Gigha, meant that for the total sum of £49,000, for the first time so far as we know one proprietor owned the whole Island.

For over fifty years Gigha remained in the possession of the Scarlett Family. In 1880 William James Scarlett succeeded his father and on William James' death his son William James Yorke Scarlett became Laird of Gigha and remained so till it was sold in 1919.

As we go along we shall examine the influence on the Island of these successive proprietors but, now having provided a background for the story of the people of Gigha we must retrace our steps to find out what was happening to them during all these changes in the ownership of their Island.

Leim Farm (c. 1908)

Chapter 5—The Minister's account

Not only did Gigha have a new owner during the last twenty years of the eighteenth Century, the Parish of Gigha and Cara also had a fresh minister appointed in 1791. This was the Reverend William Fraser whose personality will dominate the next two chapters of our exploration. In 1791 he wrote, for the General Assembly of the Church, a *Statistical Account* of his Parish in which he gave meticulous details about the social and economic life of the Island. During his ministry the earliest extant Kirk Session Book was kept with a wealth of detail. In this chapter I suggest we look at his *Statistical Account,* leaving the affairs of the Parish itself to the next one. The Account will provide us with a framework for our picture, the Records give it a lively third dimension.

The Reverend Fraser began by noting that over 600 people lived on the Island and that the number had increased in the previous few years. Each family had an average of three children while about 22 families lived in each clachan or farm-village. The days of tenant farmers in the fifteen farms on Gigha had not yet arrived. " Instead of occupying each farm in common as formerly they are now beginning to divide one farm from another by Dykes," he told the Assembly. " Also they are beginning to subdivide each farm so that each tenant may have his marked off and enclosed."

" On these fields they are beginning to grow Hay for Winter feed, encouraged by the example of John McNeill." This would gradually wipe out the wasteful custom of slaughtering in the Autumn all but a few beasts. In addition they grew Oats, Potatoes and Barley, using ploughs each drawn by four horses. " There are 24 ploughs on the Island," he wrote " each drawn by four horses." As they could not grow a Wheat crop they used the oats as their staple diet and in addition consumed much of their prolific potato crop themselves. Lacking much arable land they grew the latter in " Lazy beds " in the Irish fashion, that is planting the Potatoes close together and covering the whole bed with decaying turf and earth. Although they did export some Oats, one of the Island's most lucrative exports, right through the next century was Potatoes which the Irish came and fetched for seed. In fact legend on Gigha is strong that the Irish also wanted Gigha Potatoes, which were particularly large, to put on top of their own bags for market! This of course provided some ready money – always a scarce commodity on the Island. Not that much was required as nobody needed to buy much. Still, rents had to be paid and certain commodities, like Salt and Iron, Tar and Rope, Leather and some Flour had to be imported for money. Many of the Irish came to Cuddyport, *Port nan Cuiclainnean,* away over on the West Coast for their potatoes and one inhabitant still remembers that the potato store was in a shed where the present Cuddyport Cottage now stands.

From the Barley of course *Aquae Vitae* was distilled, a process forbidden to all but the Proprietor. In 1791 Mr. Fraser wrote that "there is one Distiller on the Island " but I am far from convinced that he was correct in this assertion because tales are still current on the Island, complete with names, of less law-abiding residents of Gigha who threw their whisky making paraphernalia into *Tar an Tarb,* the Loch of the Bull, when the Excise men came, while another fled to Glasgow and was never seen again on Gigha – this at the very end of the last century, within living memory!

The Barley, of course, could also be added to vegetables which " may be raised in great abundance and perfection," the soil being good and neither moles nor any continuance of frost to counteract the activities of the gardener. At least I can vouch for the accuracy of this statement. Even today no soup compares with Gigha broth made from home grown ingredients!

Whether the people of Gigha exported *Aquae Vitae,,* Butter or Cheese we don't know but Aquae Vitae sold at 14/- a gallon while a " stone of Cheese (24lbs.) sold at 5/- and a stone of

Butter was 10/-." This is the earliest reference I have found to Cheese making on the Island so I wish the minister had told us if it were exported.

Two other crops were harvested: Flax and Kelp. Of Flax " a good quantity is raised yearly and sold in yarn at 2/- the spindle." When discussing wages we shall learn that " a sowing of Flax seed " was part of a maid-servant's wages an ., as I have found no trace of a field where flax was grown I conclude that people grew it in their garden to augment the family income. It would appear probable that they worked the Flax and wove it on the Island because in 1841 two men did " Wool and Linen weaving," in 1851 they were noted simply as " weavers " but the occupation is not again mentioned in the *Census Returns*.

Finally we come to Kelp.[1] Cut from deep water at low tide the seaweed is burnt in a kiln when the resultant alkaline is exported for use in the glass-making industry. The men engaged in the process usually were provided with crofts near the shore. All these factors governed the Kelp industry of Gigha. In the first place, although we believe that a considerable quantity of Kelp grows on the rocks off Gigha, " with a North wind the tide seldom rises more than 5 or 6 feet — with a South wind there is hardly a foot of difference between high and low water — this prevents the manufacture of Kelp to any great extent — it has not been cut annually, but at the end of every three years, the quantity of Kelp may be about 21 tons at every cutting." So, although the Gigha Kelp cutters earned little they were at least spared the hardships facing Kelp harvesters elsewhere.

Even if it wasn't a major occupation, the Kelp manufacture for glass does recall that, according to Mr. Fraser, Gigha had a flourishing connection with a glass works in Dumbarton where a good quantity of the silver sand from Gigha's shores was sent. I think we can still find a relic of the Kelp work today in the Drumeonbeg Crofts. For all the other crofts on Gigha, the Smithy Croft, the Mill Croft and so on we can find a reason but, until I read about Kelp I often wondered why these Crofts at Drumeonbeg existed. I should like to suggest that they were the Kelp workers' abodes.

Furthermore it is just possible that the field at the Ferry may have acquired its name, *Achnahia*, the Field of the Kiln, because there the Kelpers brought in their crop, which would be the best place to do so anyway, and there they had their Kiln. Of course this may have referred to a Lime Kiln but the Field's proximity to a good shore, a good export harbour and the possible dwelling places of the Kelpers suggests that it was here they carried out their work.

So much then, at least in the meantime, about Gigha's crops. We turn to the *Account* to see what Mr. Fraser had to say about the animals and stock of the farms.

" Black Cattle and Horses — the Island of Gigha was formerly divided into thirty merklands, to each of which 14 cows and 4 horses were allowed but, Mr. Fraser added ' the number of black cattle and horses at present far exceeds this number."

Black cattle, animals being fattened for the markets, mainly of England, formed, at that time, a very valuable export of all the Highlands and Islands.[2] So far as Islay, Colonsay, Jura and Gigha were concerned the beasts required further fattening before going South, so dealers used to come round, buy up cattle, transport them to the mainland *en route* for the markets of Falkirk, Kilmichael Glassary or Dumfries whence they were sent to graze on Lowland farms before finally going to England. Prices rose steeply during the Napoleonic Wars as much meat was required for the Navy. In 1763 Hebridean Cattle were fetching two guineas each at Falkirk while, when the *Account* was written the price was around £4 an animal. Thus Mr. Fraser's figure of the export from Gigha of 120 black cattle a year meant an income, from cattle alone, of some £300. As the rent value of the whole Island was " about £700 annually " this was indeed a valuable source of revenue.

The men of Gigha, however found one drawback, at least, to this trade. The dealers who came round and ' bought' the beasts usually paid in the promissary notes, the idea being they would pay the money when the cattle had been sold and they returned for the next lot.[3] Needless to say this was not entirely a returned for the next lot. Needless to say this was not entirely a satisfactory arrangement! Apart from anything else, even when bills were eventually paid, the actual money was not always genuine. A great deal of counterfeit money was circulating all over the country at that time anyway and, when we read the Kirk Session Minutes we'll find that Gigha had a good share of what they termed 'bad money,' much of which found its way into the Church funds.

Another difficulty was, of course, the safe transport of the animals across Gigha Sound " in sailing and rowing boats mainly open, not decked at all, single masted but with heavy oars to help in calm weather — the ferrying took several days, the cattle already ferried across on the mainland resting and feeding on the rich pastures in the Kintyre coast." [4]

I always think of this when I read about the alleged theft by the Macleans in the 17th Century when they were said to have raided Gigha and removed 500 cattle and 2000 sheep to the mainland.[5] This must have required a truly mammoth transportation and I cannot imagine that they managed it without first massacring large numbers of Gigha people; a crime which is not mentioned at that time.

Concerning sheep we find that " hitherto sheep have not been kept to any great extent on the Island." I wonder about the 2000 stolen by the Macleans? Did this discourage the sheep-rearing farmers? Mr. Fraser thought this was because the people of Gigha believed that the keeping of sheep in some way impeded the growth of Black Cattle. However, as they erected more dykes to keep them apart more were being reared especially in the " many peninsulas which can be easily enclosed," so that they were beginning to keep a good number " for the convenience of mutton and the improvement of the finer kinds of wool."

I must admit here that the question of enclosure of land for sheep rearing, which caused so much distress in other parts of the Highlands, is by no means one of the clearer parts of the history of Gigha, and one which I have, despite much searching not been able to find out about. Certainly it did not take place until the mid-nineteenth Century, if then, as the population did not fall dramatically till between 1860 and 1870, a point which we shall investigate in the Nineteenth Century chapter when we shall find that, possibly on the peninsulas, particularly on the Kinerarach end of the Island, sheep were extensively reared.

So far as meat for their own consumption was concerned as well as mutton and beef, the Islander had at least some poultry of all kinds. Mr. Fraser tells us " A goose sells at 1/6, a good hen at 6d., a chicken at 3d., and a dozen eggs at 2d." For the rest " As few predators lived on the Island the only prolific wild animals are rabbits."

From all of which we know that at the end of the Eighteenth Century men and women on Gigha reared animals for their own subsistence, gaining money by exporting mainly black cattle. Of their crops they exported a quantity of potatoes and some oatmeal and barley using the remainder of those for themselves. On the whole none of this is unusual for an Island at that time but it does make inference from other Islands unnecessary for Gigha.

Obviously rearing animals and growing crops were only two of the occupations of the people of Gigha: a large number of them made their living at 'The Fishing.' Both Cod and Herring were fished commercially by boats which went to far fields and were absent for many weeks. The Herring Fishing, in particular, worried the minister:— " Sixty or more of the Islanders who engaged in this lucrative business, being away from home from June till January each year were rarely married and so, when they were at home, lived with relatives where they exerted a bad influence as they had no specific work to do." Not only that but they usually returned to Gigha with money in their pockets where " from the habits they acquire aboard they are not inclined to work hard ashore."

Apart from the commercial fishermen almost every family on the Island had a boat, either to cross to the Mainland or else to fish the Haddock, Lythe, Mackerel, Skate and Dog Fish which abounded just off the shore, or for that matter off the rocks: " To catch the Mackerel which frequent the sunken rocks round the shore a fishing rod is used with a hair line and a hook mounted with a Goose or a Seagull's white feather." Simplest of all " Cuddies (young Saithe) are taken from the rocks with a small hook or pin bended in the form of a hook."

At Cuddyport, on the West coast below Ardlammy, " everyone fishes for himself except when the whole party joins in pounding the bait, the flesh of a black Whelk and then throwing it into the sea when these beautiful small fish make their appearance in large numbers, darting at once from all directions like the radii of a circle." I like to sit sometimes facing the Atlantic at *Port nan Cuidainnean* thinking of the merry fishing parties when the men, women and children came with their " rods " with bent pins, bashed the whelks with stones, threw them into the sea, and pulled out the silver fish and laid them on the grass. I imagine the scene with the sun shining and a gentle breeze blowing, everyone jostling for a good position, arguing just whose pile of cuddies was whose, bare feet scampering around on the rough grass, the more adventurous perching on the out-jutting rocks, mothers calling caution, men vying with each other.

As the sun was setting in a blaze of red and purple over Jura they all trekked homewards, to Leim, Ardlammy, Kinerarach and Ardminish to make their *Savas,* that delicious fish soup made by boiling the Cuddy flesh in milk with a lump of butter and a couple of onions. The only imported ingredient would be the Salt. Even the black iron pot would have been fashioned in the Smiddy at Ardminish as would the *Swee.* Everyone cooked on an open fire with a *Swee.* Vertically by the side of the open fire a fixed iron stanchion had an iron projecting arm which could be swung over the fire. On it would be hung hooks of differing lengths depending on how near the fire you wanted your pot to be. Into your soup of course you could put any other fish including any of " the abundance of shell-fish which surround the shores."

Besides Farmers and Fishermen certain other specialists were necessary. These Mr. Fraser lists under " Handycrafts — men etc." For instance he wrote that no less than five weavers worked on the Island. To make the cloth up were four Tailors who worked for 8d. a day and their keep while the shoemaker charged 1/- for making a pair of shoes in his own house but only 6d. if he were given his maintenance. In addition three Apprentices worked with these men but which learnt with which trade he didn't tell us. Two " Boat Carpenters " made boats while one Mason sufficed for building and one distiller (officially) and two innkeepers catered for the leisure side of life which would be enlivened by the one fiddler and the two pipers. As in later centuries life was not all ploughing and reaping, weaving and fishing on Gigha, far from it, they had their gay moments as well!

In case you are thinking that most people lived on farms and earned no money I hasten to add that many were employed at a wage. " The common wage of men labourers is 8d. a day, summer and winter. A ploughman is hired from December to the end of May, at £2 10/- besides two pairs of shoes, a planting of two pecks of potatoes, sowing of a pint of flax seed, and maintenance. A man servant is hired from the latter end of August till the harvest is finished at about £2 15/- with a pair of shoes and his maintenance, a maid servant for the same gets £1 10/- with shoes and maintenance; common men servants are hired at the rate of £4 10/- a year and maintenance; maid servants at £2 10/- with maintenance, shoes and flax-seed sowing; herd boys from 15/- to 20/-."

As in all such communities two essential specialists serving the Island enjoyed, if that is the word, special conditions; the Blacksmith and the Miller. Each had his own Croft where he could keep animals and grow a few crops for his own household. The Crofts are still there today although Gigha has neither Smiddy nor a working Mill. These crofts are still worked by the descendants of former Smiths and Millers.

Take the Smiddy first. The last Smith on Gigha, Archie Bannatyne, now lives in a new house built on the site of his old Smiddy. It would be reasonable to assume that the work done by Archie Bannatyne and his father, Neil, differed little from what James Dewar the Smith did in Mr. Fraser's day. The Smith, Mr. Bannatyne told me, made all the iron goods required on the Island: pots, pails, farm implements, iron chains, anchors and of course the Swees for cooking. Not only did he shoe all the horses and fashion much of the harness but he also finished off the wooden wheels made by the carpenter.

Mr. Bannatyne took me outside his house to show me, lying in the tidy grass verge, the large stone wheel with a hole for the hub and radiating grooves to hold the wooden wheel while the Smith carefully put the red-hot band of iron round the rim: red-hot, just the temperature to grip properly when cold but not too hot to burn the wood.

Another very important part of the Smiddy, which I am sure was in use in Mr. Fraser's day is the old anvil which Neil, Archie Bannatyne's son, has in his garden up at Cairnvickoye. This venerable relic of the old Gigha was last used to shoe a working horse in May 1965.

The Mill Croft we have already dealt with. Now it is time to look at the Reverend Fraser's remarks about John McNeill's attempts to improve the buildings of Gigha as well as erecting new ones. Several new houses, the minister noted " have recently been built on the Island. Within these four years two new public houses, each consisting of two garrets and a malt kiln and granary, all with slated roofs have been erected." It seems unlikely that such excellent houses have disappeared. Only two houses on Gigha today correspond to Mr. Fraser's description: the *Gigha Hotel* and the *Post Office and Shop*. True both have been internally completely modernised but, externally they correspond to Mr. Fraser's description, remembering that in the eighteenth Century public house meant just that — a house for public use of some kind.

Little doubt exists that the *Gigha Hotel* has always been, so far as we know, the one Inn on the Island. Before the recent reorganisation it was declared to be a scheduled building which is why the external appearance remained unchanged during the recent extensive modernisation.

That brings us to the second of Mr. McNeill's ' new ' buildings, the one which is today the Post Office and Shop, but which from 1791 or so till 1912 was Gigha School. The Master lived on the ground floor while the one very large long room above became the schoolroom where generations of Gigha children did their lessons. In a later chapter[6] we'll see how it has been altered

51

and meet someone who went to school there but meantime let's see what we know about Gigha School in the time of Mr. Fraser. He, himself, wrote in his *Account* that " 55 boys and 10 girls attended the school — 8 of them learnt Arithmetic and 32 English – the rest were beginners."

A curious account of the situation is in a document found among the Campbell papers by the Argyll Archivist, Mr. Murdo MacDonald.[7] This is dated 1784 and is a Petition from John McNeill Esq., of Gigha to the Synod of Argyll. It " Showeth — that the Petitioner has been at pains and expense in procuring a proper schoolmaster for the Parish of Gigha and having found one who teaches Book-keeping, Navigation, Reading, English and Gaelic, Writing, Arithmetic and Church Music with success that the School is in a flourishing state and the number of scholars in general between 90 and 100.

" In this small Parish there are no fewer than 35 widows, most of whom have children at the School. Two thirds of the scholars are children of those widows and of sailors some of whom have been impressed on board the Royal Navy."

" The Petitioner, anxious to promote the success of the school and thereby afford the means of education and Religious Knowledge to many poor children, flatters himself that the very Reverend Synod will so far co-operate as to give £20 or at least £15 towards the encouragement of the said School and as an aid to build a proper Schoolhouse out of the Vacant Stipend which has been paid to the Synod out of the Parish of Gigha and Cara for the last five years." Signed John McNeill. Gigha 26th July 1794.

Unfortunately this intriguing document is, so far only a solitary one which has been found in an unclassified bundle of Argyll Synod papers and we don't know what happened. The request seems reasonable enough. The vacancy had indeed occurred for five years before Mr. Fraser's appointment. The ' learned ' schoolmaster whom John McNeill had procured was John Galbraith who was also Session Clerk for many years. We first meet him in the first list of Elders in 1799 and he was still

Session Clerk the last time the Office was mentioned in the Kirk Session Records in 1827. The 'proper Schoolmaster' must have indeed been one of the Grand Old Men of Gigha!

So far as other new houses built by Mr. McNeill were concerned Mr. Fraser noted that he "caused 14 other houses to be built — 5 of which are slated." This would leave us to assume that the other houses were thatched, even the new ones. Still they would be solid enough being built of stone — "an abundance of whin and grey-stone fit for building handsome houses was got from the slag quarry stones which make good pavement floors or hearth stones."

As so often, just when we think everything is falling nicely into place a mystery appears. This time it surrounds "the old Manse." Mr. Fraser remarked, "Mr. McNeill of Gigha is making repairs and offices about the old manse which he occupies as a temporary mansion house." Where was this "old manse?" and if the principal proprietor was occupying this where was Mr. Fraser's Manse?

The Manse, as it exists near the Ferry today, was erected in 1816 so that can be discounted at this stage as a manse in the Eighteenth Century. On the principle that the Manse is generally near the Church one would expect the "old" manse to be near Keill, in fact where a later proprietor built Achamore House, which therefore we might consider to be on the site of a much older house. Certainly we shall find grounds, in the Kirk Session Records, for thinking that John McNeill had his own farm up at Achamore. Perhaps even more important than where his residence was is the fact that this reference informs us that John McNeill lived on the Island. Earlier Lairds may well have done so although we have no proof of the fact but it is true that, with a few exceptions, and these for short periods, all succeeding proprietors have resided for a good part of the year on their property and taken a close personal interest in its welfare and viability.

As to Mr. Fraser's dwelling place: available evidence indicates it was where South Drumachro farmhouse stands today. Several of the Kirk Session meetings in Mr. Fraser's time were held at "South Drumachro" or simply "Drumachro."

We have already noted that John McNeill encouraged the growing of hay for winter feed, and tried to persuade the people to enclose parts of their land and give up the shared fields of the old run-rig system. He built a certain number of " good houses " although obviously these were outnumbered by the older houses mostly built by the inhabitants themselves by the simple process of erecting four stone walls and adding a thatched roof all enclosing enough space in which the family could live together with their livestock, possibly through a partition. We'll examine the ruins of some of these houses later.

One of John McNeill's most beneficial improvements was the road. " From the Harbour at Gigulum Sound, there is an excellent line of carriage road, finished half way to the North end of the Island to the great convenience of the inhabitants, who are now beginning to use carts, of which there are now six on the Island." This vital improvement the minister attributed to the Proprietor because, according to Mr. Fraser, although everybody was supposed to do statute work on the roads in those days, while parliament was required to pay 1/- in the pound of rent for road making, " the money thus raised goes to the great lines of road on the mainland — nothing of this money can be applied to other places till these have been completed, consequently the road on Gigha has been carried on at the expense of the Proprietor."

It is also worth noting too that none of Mr. McNeill's " improvements " in the way of enclosures or dyke building led to many people leaving the Island as happened elsewhere. In fact, as Mr. Fraser noted, the opposite seemed to be the case, the population was increasing which would appear to show his tenants were profitting by his attempts to improve their lot.

Two things were lacking on this otherwise flourishing Island. In the first place fuel was extremely scarce, and in the second place no doctor lived on the Island.

So far as fuel was concerned Mr. Fraser recorded that, in view of the prohibitive cost of transporting coal to the Island the only fuel here is peats which are so scarce that the proprietors are under the necessity of allowing the inhabitants to cut away the surface of pasture and even of meadow ground. Once a year the Mill Loch was drained when the people could cut peat. Incidentally the grain at the Mill was dried until the Mill itself ceased to function by peat burned under the great iron grating in the floor. In Mr. Fraser's opinion the Proprietor ought to plant trees but his advice went unheeded for another hundred years.

The absence of a resident doctor is still a disadvantage on the Island although modern transport and the presence of a highly trained nurse together with regular visits of the mainland doctor do compensate somewhat. In Mr. Fraser's day the nearest doctor was at Campbeltown so that " Although the residents of these Islands are uncommonly healthy yet want of a surgeon is still felt in accidental circumstances." The kind of accidents he was thinking about we find in the Kirk Session Records. For instance in applying for poor relief was a " poor widow who has the burden of her son Neil who has for some time been incapable by reason of a bruise he got under a load of potatoes and being disabled by a rupture." Another casualty was Flora who had " lost her sight in the Harvest."

Just before Mr. Fraser left Gigha a serious epidemic was rife and a " surgeon " called Mr. Brown was summoned from Campbeltown and paid for by the Kirk Session. Mr. Brown came only once so I feel he must have produced a cure. According to the Kirk Session Record of the occurrence " the main cause is uncleanness allied to people hiding the fact that they have got the disease which is particularly undesirable if a family is involved." This all cost the Session £1 for the surgeon's fee and 4/- for his transport to the Island. Only the Kirk Session could afford this sort of money.

Mr. Fraser concluded his *Account* with some general remarks of which one of the most significant was " accustomed to certain mode of labour for the support of his family never attempts any greater exertion when this has been achieved. There is no market at hand where ready money can be got for the produce of the ground and therefore no incitement to raise a greater quantity than serves for family consumption and payment of rent." As we progress through the Nineteenth and on to the Twentieth Centuries bear in mind that very perceptive statement about the lack of a market where ready money can be got. Narrow it still further to the operative words "ready money." This I believe is the key to the economic and social life on Gigha. In contrast to people on the Mainland the inhabitants of Gigha had little need of much cash nor did they think much about ready money till this present century, as we shall see. We must follow up the complementary implication that a time comes on every Gigha Farm, Croft or Cottage when the produce of the Island will not suffice for everyone so that some of necessity or inclination must leave the Island to seek a livelihood elsewhere, like Neil and Grisella McNeill in the early Eighteenth Century.

So much for the future. Now we press on with a sound knowledge of the social and economic background of Gigha to see what the records of the Kirk Session have to tell us about the more personal side of life.

Chapter 6—The early Kirk Session book

In its modern form the Parish of Gigha and Cara dates from January 22nd 1726 when the two islands were formally disjointed from Killean Parish and declared to be a separate parish. The first minister was the Reverend Neil Simpson who was succeeded by William Mowat who in turn gave place to Dugald MacDougall. Of these we know nothing except that Mr. MacDougall took the Records with him when he left and ' mislaid ' them. Thus the first Kirk Session Records we have date from the time of the Reverend Fraser who was appointed in 1791 although I suspect he was on the Island before that as he knew so much about it and a few notes exist in the Session Book prior to his official appointment.

When I first read the thick volume of handwritten pages chronicling the cases of Sabbath Breaking, Calumny and Immorality, the lists of ministers and elders and the moneys given to the ' Poors ' I knew I had found a treasure chest of information for our studies; not so much in what was recorded but from the implications behind the various reports. Soon I began to realise that its limitations resulted partly from the fact that the Session Clerk did not record any facts which he considered everyone knew anyway so that many of the cases are, to say the least of it, obscure. Moreover, after about 1802 reports become more scanty until shortly only the date of the Communion Sunday is noted together with a few cases.

The very first paragraph hints at a very important milestone in the Church life of Gigha. Dated 20th February 1785 it records that a Collection is to be taken towards the S.P.C.K.'s project of translating the Old Testament into the Gaelic Language. What sum was collected is not stated but the translation was made so that the people of the Western Isles could read the Old

Testament for themselves. It may have been this translation which sparked off what appears to be an increased interest in Church affairs.

The most important person to foster such an interest was of course the minister. After the departure of Mr. MacDougall with the Records one Samuel Peat was presented to the living by the Duke of Argyll and John McNeill. Presented he may have been, but the people of Gigha knew their rights and objected very strongly to his appointment due to his " lack of proficiency in the Gaelic tongue." This contention was upheld, after examination of Mr. Peat by both the Presbytery of Kintyre and the Synod of Argyll. Five years later when Mr. Peat was appealing to the General Assembly John McNeill took a hand and wrote to the Synod " the situation renders it peculiarly hard to be so long without a minister to dispense the Ordinances of religion on Gigha." As a result in 1791 the Reverend Fraser was presented and duly appointed.

On the face of it Mr. Fraser's ministry was a well disciplined time. For the next ten years, till September 1801 frequent Session Meetings were held, sometimes four or five a week, dispatching, with patient thoroughness, all the business that came before them. The Session was well organised and the poor cared for. Efficient Mr. Fraser undoubtedly was but subsequent events lead us to question his popularity among his parishioners.

Suddenly, in 1801, we read of an extraordinary event when the Presbytery of Kintyre visited Gigha to " examine the minister's complaints." That man, whom the people of the Island had won for themselves only ten years previously complained that his glebe " was at a considerable distance," that his manse " was so uncomfortable as to endanger his health and that of his family " that he had " nowhere to keep a cow or a horse " and that " when his well ran dry he was denied the use of a neighbouring well to get a supply of clean water." The Presbytery examined all these complaints and found that he " suffered from what seemed to the Presbytery to be a studied system of oppression " and advised him to leave the Island. This he did " after suitable and affectionate advices " in 1802.

Much of this could be explained by the fact that his Manse was at South Drumachro[1] although the matter of the well running dry is odd because the South Drumachro well is known as being one of the more dependable wells on the Island. We can conclude only that Mr. Fraser's zeal outran his discretion. It is a strange thought that it is largely due to his excessive zeal that you and I know so much about Gigha at the turn of the century!

The incumbencies of his two successors were very unhappy and it was not till the Reverend James Curdie was appointed in 1827 that the Church on Gigha seems to have sailed once more on an even keel under this scholarly and discreet man.

From the Ministers we turn to consider the Elders who, of course, in theory at least, were chosen by the congregation. Their duties in the Parish were set out in May 1794, after a particularly bad case of Sabbath Breaking: " The Elders will see to it that the people of their several districts go to Church. They must examine the conduct of their people on the Lord's Day and use every means to prevent irregularities." Heads of families, too had duties: "they must attend Divine Service, keep due order in their families at home and oblige them to render an account of their behaviour while out of their parents' or master's sight." The Session considered that " Without such due observance of the Sabbath there is an end to all religious institutions, all order and reformation. In consequence of the ignorance which unavoidably follows the neglect of religious duties the people will become careless and lax in their morals and the greatest degeneracy and deprivation of matters will ensue."

In May 1794 each Elder was allotted a particular clachan as his responsibility which provides us with much interesting information as well as the names of Elders. Some had " other " duties: John McNeill was Ruling Elder, Neil Galbraith " the old " (at one time three of that name were Elders known as One, Two and Three) while John Galbraith was Schoolmaster and Session Clerk.

Otherwise the list reads: " Neil Galbraith for Ceann-ear-ireach,[2] that farm and Garb Acha[3] and on Sunday Carn-mhic-aoi;[4]

Neil Smith and Donald M'Intaggart, Ardelay; Malcolm Blue the Miller, Ardacha and Knock-a-Mullian;[5] Archibald Smith, Ardlammy (which appears to be narrowly looked after and negligent in attendance at Church and saunter about on the Lord's Day by which other people are prevented from going to Church); Malcolm Galbraith, Drumyeoun and the Crofts of Ardmeanish; Doug Smith, Ardmeanish, Tigh a Ru and Achaveanish; Neil Galbraith, Keill (he will easily keep these people in order); Lachlan Mc Lachlan, Shansrioch[6] where he lives and Leim; Neil Galbraith, South Drumachro, North Drumachro and Cara but any elder may admonish *anywhere*."

Regrettably this is the only list of elders we have. Occasionally " new " elders are recorded as being appointed but it is impossible to make comprehensive lists. Certainly we are not again given lists of special districts so whether it became traditional or was given up we don't know.

Seeking enlightment, as well as entertainment, we now look at some of the cases which were reported as coming before the Session; cases of Disorder, Calumny and Immorality.

First of all take Disorder which meant doing something during the time of Divine Service other than sitting in Church. What mattered was not so much *what* you were doing as *when* you were doing it! Quite the most intriguing such incident happened on Sunday 19th February 1786 on the wild west shore of Leim. " On this day," we read " was convened on Leim Shore a great number of the people of this Parish during the time of Divine Service — waiting what wreckage might be cast ashore by the waves and behaving themselves in a riotous and indecent fashion." The Session agrees that " such contempt of Public Worship is highly censurable and in order to discover and convict those guilty of such outrages they order and summon by name some of the male inhabitants to attend the next meeting of the Session."

Then follows an account, not only of the next meeting but of several others to consider the matter. This careful examination of witnesses and accused, the weighing up of the evidence and the eventual meting out of punishment forms one of the most notable features of the Session's proceedings. Sometimes they met on as many as six days about one case. In fact, on one occasion they took so long to come to a verdict that the accused had left the Island!

About the Leim Shore affair they duly interviewed several inhabitants who all arrived with expressions of injured innocence and excellent excuses for their presence on Leim Shore co-incidentally with wood from a wreck being washed ashore. John Innes declared he had " been following some cattle who had strayed when he saw a great number of people strolling about the Shore and handling some timber which had come ashore." He went on to say that " Adam of Kinerarach was claiming the timber and also Lachlan McNeill of Leim and they were having some debates about the subject."

Lachlan Galbraith, feeling particularly ill-used, pointed out that " I was sitting at home in my house not having any shoes to go out in. On a girl coming to my door she told me about the throng securing timber so I went to their assistance." He had been joined by several others, one of whom had gone " to see a friend of my wife's who was sick."

Unluckily for all those worthy folk the Elders them-selves were Gigha men and were not in any way impressed by these tales so they duly meted out punishment which varied from fines of around 2/6 to a public reprimand. All fines were given to the ' poors.' John had to pay an extra 10/- for " Speaking disrespect-fully about the Elder."

The fines, we were told were to be given to the ' poors ' for whom the Church was responsible. At this time, so far as I can gather the indigent poor on Gigha numbered about eight but the trouble is that the book which the Session had ordered for the Accounts was either never bought or else has been lost. One did did exist in 1840 when Mr. Curdie referred to it but when it was bought and used we don't know.

The ' reprimanded in Church ' was a usual punishment those days when convicted culprits had to sit in a special place in Church to be ' reprimanded.' This part of the punishment was much more disliked than paying a fine so that, when one offender in 1794 suggested paying 5/- instead, the Elders seized on the idea and, in future a payment of 10/- could be made to escape a "reprimand." Considering these fines were the backbone of the poor relief this was indeed a welcome idea!

If you think again of the Leim affair let me point out that "knocking out of iron bolts from the larger pieces of timber" was no Sunday morning amusement but was a deadly serious necessity. Mr. Fraser has already told us of the shortage of wood for building or fuel so obviously anyone wanting to have a good fire or build a new house or, for that matter, repair the one he had, then the large planks of ship timber would indeed be worth a fine or a public reprimand. In fact this shortage of timber lasted till this present century when people still living on the Island have told me of their fathers and brothers salvaging timber from the shores of Gigha. The fault committed that Sunday at Leim was a sin only because it was being committed on Sunday — and you'll notice Lachlan Galbraith who was himself an elder was on the shore.

Listen now to the Tale of the Hanks of Yarn! This attracted my attention when I read the preamble, written in 1794 "when young women forgot the delicacy of their sex and break through the restraints of modesty and shame to gratify a vicious pleasure, what can be expected of them in advanced life? And when old women encourage others in debauchery what reformation can be looked for?"

You may well wonder what orgiastic rites had been going on on Creag Bhan or down at Gigulum Shore. In any case remember that whatever the "vicious pleasure" was, it was being enjoyed on a Sunday otherwise it would not have come under the jurisdiction of the Session. What happened was that on Sunday 4th May 1794 a lady called Mary visited her friend Margaret at Ardmeanish. To her she gave "a hank of yearn to buy some whiskey by way of a play it being Peace Sunday. The said Margaret (alias Maggie) went to the Public House for a mutchkin of Whiskey of which they took two drams apiece." They may have had only two drams apiece but as a mutchkin is just over a pint they must have been fairly large drams. From here the party snowballed, more hanks of yarn were acquired from friends who joined the party which, by this time had begun to move around the Island, gathering "guests" as it went. In fact it finally fetched up as far away as Leim. Some time later Mary and Margaret arrived back in Ardmeanish where, they pleaded "they had been so drunk as scarcely to know anything that passed." Mary deposed that she had been put to bed in an intoxicated state." Everyone accused in the whiskey party admitted that this had happened during Divine Service. It took the Session so long to interview everyone and sort it all out that no sentence could be passed as Mary had "left the country."

So hanks of yarn were negotiable. Moreover the Inn remained open during Divine Service so was the Inn Chargekeeper excused from attendance? Above all Divine Service lasted a long time evidently. Before we discuss that here's another sin two men and their friends committed which gives us the same impression. In July 1799 two men were accused of spending Sunday collecting oats "from John McNeill's store at Achamore" and ferrying it over to Kilberry while also during Divine Service another set were doing exactly the same, only this time the oats were going to Jura. I may say the Ferryman Donald McQuilkan was exonerated because he had been 'Coerced.' This incidentally gives us the first name of a ferryman on Gigha. Again it tells us that John had an "oats store" at Achamore, a point which will become important in our next chapter.

Apart from the fact that all these lads were engaged in what would ordinarily be their legal occupations but which had become illegal during Divine Service it would seem that they could have done it before or after Church. Not so! In an invaluable book by J. M. Ross called *Four Centuries of Scottish Worship* I find that between 1769 and 1869 the Morning Service lasted from 10.30 a.m. to 12.30 p.m. while the Afternoon Service went on from 2 p.m. till about 4 p.m. One reason for the length of the Services was that the Sermon, preached without notes, lasted anything between one and one and a half hours. The Psalms were 'lined,' that is, the Precentor said a line, which the congregation repeated, then he said the next and they repeated it and so on, a process that could last a good twenty minutes. Prayers were *ex tempore* so lasted as long as the minister found subjects to pray about. Besides all this, sinners had to be reprimanded, a matter which took just as long as necessary. So, you see Mary and Margaret and their friends had time to drink plenty of mutchkins and the oats ferrying lads had a nice quiet day to work in. The timber crashing in on to Leim Shore might have gone out on the next tide!

As I went on reading in the later years I couldn't help regretting that the most illuminating cases belong to the time before Mr. Fraser left. I can't believe that none occurred. Something tells me Mr. Curdie played it more coolly!

At the first reading the Calumny cases appear tedious: meeting after meeting was devoted to finding out whether Mary had called Catherine a whore or not the Session ' finds ' for one or other, someone pays a fine, perhaps both, for upsetting the peace.

When I considered further I realised that the apparent plethora of cases is due to the number of meetings the Elders would devote to one case. Witnesses either " heard someone else " retail the alleged story or they had " been from home " when it was said and so on and so forth. In fact nobody would ever own up to anything about the supposed calumny. Sometimes someone did, volubly, but then you find he was a relation of one or other party. When I counted up I discovered that, in fifteen years, before Mr. Fraser left, only six cases came before the Session, and, when I consider that well over four hundred adults lived on the Island this does not appear excessive. On the other hand, in 1786, the Session Clerk noted " We deplore the number of cases of calumny which come before us and, in future such cases will be very severely dealt with. On the whole I sympathise with John Galbraith when he found it too laborious to sharpen his quills and mix up more ink powder to write out all the details of the tiffs of the Parish.

The point to remember is that the Elders were " main tainers of concord among neighbours " and furthermore, " if discord arises they must first try appeal and, only if that fails are they to bring the matter to the Session." When we come to considering the Sacramental Sabbath we shall find that, before the annual event the Ministers and Elders had to ensure that all those communicating were "in love and charity with their neighbours."

Some of the cases are in themselves amusing and indicates fires below the surface as in the case of William who in August 1786 told the Session that he was "sitting quietly at my own front door in Keil when John came and gave me very abusive language. He threatened me in such a manner that I was obliged to fly for my life." He went on to point out, at some length, "I look on myself as still in danger from the hatred and malice of John." Several witnesses were called by William, many of whom seem to have been his relatives. In the end John was found guilty of "noisy and outrageous behaviour" for which he had to apologise publicly before the congregation. The only apparent reason for this verdict was the non-appearance of John to answer the charge. What tale lies beneath the tip of this fiery ice-berg?

The mysteries of John and William are as nothing compared with the voluminous case of Meran and Mary, pages and pages of this case of two Gigha ladies each of whom seemed vociferously aware that the other was a whore and a liar. It is almost impossible to make any sense of it all. For days the Elders interviewed witnesses who appeared to contradict each other about "the wickedness of John McNeill bringing the Galloichille family to the Island" and throwing in the remark "nobody seems to remember the day the shot was fired from the window of Ardmeanish House." It is the one and only time John McNeill is accused of bringing the Galloichille family to the Island, which he hadn't, so far as history relates, and where Ardmeanish House was and who fired a shot is quite outwith our present knowledge to answer. This is the supreme case in the earlier records of the Clerk putting down only a selection of facts because everyone knew what it was all about. What is even more odd is that he never recorded what finally happened. The whole thing just faded out.

The only reason I mention this tedious case at all is because it teaches us a very salutary lesson that, however much we can learn from documents or reports, we still cannot know the whole truth of the social and 'political' atmosphere of the Island. We can discover only a limited amount but still I am glad we can glance, if only for a moment, into underlying currents below the surface which we cannot penetrate.

Among the sparsely detailed calumny cases later in the century we find the most bizarre case of all which amply demonstrates this point of the dangers of thinking we know all about the problems the Elders were trying to unravel.

It was in February 1882 that two Gigha men appeared before the Session to complain that one of their fellow-Islanders was accusing them of being ' corprisers.' They stoutly denied the accusation saying that they had indeed " been the worse for drink taken " because a man, whose name they were not prepared to disclose, had asked them to " go to the Churchyard with the bodies of the sailors who had been drowned when *The Challenge* was wrecked." They wanted it to be known that they were *burying* bodies, not *raising* them. For this unpleasant duty they had been given £2 to buy drink. The Session, for some reason, did not appear to mind their being intoxicated while carrying out such a serious business. In fact they commended them for their action and their accuser was to apologise publicly in Church. When I read this I decided the Session's verdict must have been because one of the men doing the burying was " the respected grocer at Ardminish." A clear case of favouritism, I thought.

Then one day Betty and I were resting during one of our Archaeological trips. We sat on the grass idly gazing over the calm blue sea towards Gigulum. Below seals basked on the rocks by the Pier. A more peaceful and lovely scene you could hardly imagine. Suddenly Betty said " That's where *The Challenge* came in, just down there by the Coal Depot. There was a cottage there then " *Tigh Creagah* " it was called. The storm drove right up to the house. " *The Challenge* " struck one of those rocks. It was carrying a cargo of pit-props. I've heard my uncles talk about it. They waded into the sea, trying to rescue the crew but it was nearly hopeless. As they tried to pull them out the poor men begged them to leave them drown. These great wooden pit-props were pounding them to pieces with the waves. Some had lost arms, some legs, heads and bodies were crushed and bleeding. It was the most awful shipwreck ever."

No wonder the " grocer of Ardminish " and his friend got drunk before tackling the gruesome task of burying these mangled bodies'. No wonder the Elders appeared so annoyed with their accusers! The laconic reports of the Gigha Session, like the peaceful scenes on the Island can often conceal an eventful history!

To us today the whole set-up of the Immorality cases appears very strange indeed. Until you remember that behind it lay, not only a desire to maintain some sort of order on the Island but a conviction, on the part of both the Session and inhabitants that attendance at the ' Lord's Ordinances ' was necessary and that participation depended on having a clear conscience and being at one with your neighbour.

What happened in each case was that a girl came before the Session to declare that a certain named man was the father of her child. The Elders summoned him and accused him whereupon he either paid his fine quietly or else denied the allegation when the Session met again (sometimes five or six times) to call witnesses before announcing their decision and meting out punishment. By the way none of this concerned the baby who, if the couple did not marry, was brought up by the girl's family and given her surname.

Cases before the Session were those which individual elders could not settle in their districts. Take the case of Meran (almost a quarter of the girls were Meran, the others were Mary, Margaret or Anne with an occasional Flora!) A puzzled elder reported to the Session that he thought this Meran 'looked particularly bulky ' in Church recently so a couple of the worthy men of Gigha were sent to interview her at her home. She firmly denied the implied charge saying that she had " new underclothing which was bunchy." Witnesses were called at several subsequent meetings, including her girl-bedfellow who agreed Meran was not pregnant. Ultimately the Elders were proved correct and the young man whom Meran accused paid his fine and had his " reprimand."

Queer decisions were often made. On one occasion no decision seemed possible, in view of the conflicting evidence who was the father of the child so the Elders decided to " wait till the child is born when it will be clear!" Perhaps the most curious was a case where it was not the father of the child who was censured but his uncle who was severely dealt with for " allowing so young a couple to sleep together under his roof." Not only that, but this is one of the few cases when the ' culprit,' in this case the uncle, had to contribute to the upkeep of the child.

Behind some of the more macabre tales I detect a lively teen-age imagination brightening up the day-to-day life of the Island. One lass told the Elders a tale which lasted nearly a year of meetings, She complained that a married man, with whom she ' regularly slept ' had given her a box of ' large black pills ' which she had buried in the sand. He then, so she said, gave her a Pound to leave the Island which she did, in a small boat from Port nan Cuideannean. On the Mainland, Helensburgh in fact, her baby was born and christened as she had a forged marriage certificate. According to her story, which she was sticking to, her lover then wrote to her asking her to return and live with his family. This she did but was met at Tayinloan by his wife and sons who implored her to go back and offered her ten shillings to do so. As so often happens the Session Clerk got tired of the long tale, or else the matter blew over. At any rate that is the end so we never know what finally happened!

One of the tales I must admit I found not only amusing but curious concerned Samuel, a Gigha man who, on his way home from Campbeltown was storm-stayed at Ballochroy where he spent the night at the Inn sharing a bed and a room with a Gigha girl called Anne. Samuel was, in fact engaged to be married to a lady who was " the widow of the late Schoolmaster and Session Clerk." Surprisingly this lady did not seem to object; in fact it is not at all clear who did in fact bring the case to the notice of the Session.[7] At the hearing Anne and John agreed they had shared a bed but were quite clear that ' the cloaths ' had been between them all night. The story did not end there however. After a few weeks Samuel and his erstwhile betrothed were again before the Session as they had gone over to Campbeltown and got married. To do this they had forged the all-important Banns as they knew the Minister would not give them because of the case of Anne and Samuel. Even this was not the end. The Session then called for Archibald whom they said had forged the banns but he had joined

68

the Navy so all they could do was promise to deal with him should he ever return to the Island. That, so far as we know was that.

I'm not at all sure that at least some of this concern on the part of the Session was because this Anne had been before them already with an illegitimate child. In fact, by the time we hear the last of her, some five years on she has had four babies, her family have, apparently given her up, and the Session had to contribute to the upkeep of her four children. This Anne is one of three girls I found going through the Book who actually do come before the Session time after time whether from habitual wickedness, over-attractiveness or simple-mindedness I don't know. On one occasion a man was specially reprimanded because he was " well aware that Flora was young in her mind."

Now if you think you can wile away an hour or two in Edinburgh reading the juicier cases in the Session Book you will have a shock because disentangling any one story is a laborious process. The business before the Session on any one day is usually written out just as it happened so you find a case of paternity concerning say John and Anne, then on the same line a tale about a poor person, then something about a calumny. For several meetings nothing more comes up about John and Anne when suddenly they are mentioned again so you have to go back to find what it is about and if in fact it is the same John and Anne or the same John and a different Anne. Threaded through this you are trying to sort out, say the calumny case between Meran and Mary or the somewhat shaky progress of Margaret and Mary on Peace Sunday. After a time I, at least, began to get quite moithered and sympathised with old John Galbraith, the Clerk, who gave up trying to write all the details.

That is of course subjective. A more important suspicion came over me after several days of this process. I had more than an inkling why the Reverend Fraser became the victim of " a studied system of persecution." Both his Elders and his flock believed sincerely that a reasonable standard of behaviour must be maintained on the Island but I wonder if the good man knew where to be discreet and when to be severe? He had certainly forgotten how the Islanders had reacted together over Mr. Peat!

One aspect of his zeal tells us much about the attitude of the Session towards the poor. As we have seen the Treasurer's Book which the Session had ordered to be purchased in 1792 either was never got or else it is among the lost treasures of Gigha. All we are left with is a few references scattered through the Session Book if and when the Clerk thought to note them.

The most illuminating record was the result of a meeting held in 1795 at South Drumachro, which as we have seen was probably the Manse. At this South Drumachro meeting it was decided " there are others who ought to be on the Poors List who have no relations or near friends in the country and who, from advanced age or infirmity are unable to work for their bread or provide themselves with the necessities of life," accordingly two of the Elders were charged with investigation of all the Poor on Gigha. They had to examine " the state of their homes — ascertain whether their houses are properly thatched and comfortably warm and watertight — whether they have any aid from their relations, from the other tenants or from the Proprietor — and what rents are being demanded for their houses."

On November 6th 1798 two Elders reported that " their houses are tolerably comfortable. Some pay rent: John Smith (blind) Ardlammy; Meran Galbraith (Drumeonbeg); Neil Galbraith (Ardlammy); Barbara Smith who lives with her sister at Ardlammy: Dug Clark pays no rent: Mary McAllister has no home of her own but goes about the country. Meran Galbraith pays rent for her house and unable by reason of age to earn her bread and having the burden of her youngest son Neil who has for some time been incapable by reason of a bruise he got under a load of potatoes and being also disabled by a rupture; Margaret at Ardlammy, mother of blind John Smith aged upwards of 80 years is confined to bed — a real object of charity and therefore proper to be put on the Poors List." From all of this it is clear that lack of cash alone by no means constituted poverty. In fact this general attitude not only of family responsibility for the poor and for illegitimate children but a disregard for money in itself we shall find over and over again as we progress. I suppose the truth was that on Gigha people didn't need to buy very much anyway.

A CLACHAN. *Reproduced by kind permission of the artist, Edna Whyte from Old Rectory Designs, Island of Luing, Argyll.*

Between 1786 and 1804 (the only years for which we have any records) to each of eight or occasionally ten, indigent poor the Session made a more or less regular payment of quarterly sums varying between 1/6 and 3/- each person. Very seldom special payments were made: " to the old lady at Ardlammy 2/8 " or " 2/8 to Catherine Galbraith to assist her until she can join her relatives in the Low Country." (Remember that one — it may be important).

These amounts seem strange if you consider the apparent amount of money the Elders collected from fines. Unfortunately much of that money was in ' promissory notes ' which, needless to say, seldom resulted in hard cash. Not only that but, as we have already seen in the matter of Black Cattle, much ' bad money ' was in circulation all over the country at this time and some of it found its way to Gigha in payment for fish, potatoes, cattle, oats and so on. The Church suffered sadly from the result of this. In 1799 the Treasurer reported that of the £1 14s. 6½d. in the kitty he also had £6 19s. 1d. of "bad money." Again in January 1802 the balance was £9 10s. 5d. but " most of this is bad copper." In fact the overall impression I get from even the sparse reference to income is that the Church on Gigha was in a chronic state of financial difficulty. On the other hand nobody seemed to mind. Even the dues to the Church officers were conditional: 1799 " Neil Galbraith's wife has now had the trouble of the Communion Cups and Tablecloths for many years and has had no recognition for her trouble or for buying soap or for knitting pins or needles. The Session hereby agrees a sum annually of 5/- (always considering the state of the funds.)"

Besides such small fees the Elders sometimes paid for interesting items. In January 1800 they paid Malcolm Blue the Miller for making a coffin for a poor person. Malcolm charged 3/- and 5/- for the necessary wood making the sum which the Treasurer was authorised to pay 8/-. Wood you'll notice was very expensive, nearly twelve times a daily wage in harvest time.

These are the only examples we have of the Session's expenditure which is a great pity. Still we have two accounts to

71

consider which provide us with a vital clue to the highlight of Church life — the Sacramental Sunday, in the Parish of Gigha and Cara. In July 1797 we read:— " James Dewar a/c for making a Tent including timber, Iron, Workmanship — £1 16s. 6d. The Kirk Treasurer is authorised to pay this." Twelve years later, in 1810 the Kirk Treasurer paid " 4/- for one Chopin of Whisky for the Elders when fixing the Tent." In this latter account 10/6 were paid " for hire of a cart for carrying the Communion Elements from Campbeltown to Largieside and bringing them to Gigha. Pd. to Donald Galbraith for this trouble 12/-. Pd. the Bellman's wife 10/- for taking care of Linnen." Having paid this last account the Kirk Treasurer was left with a balance in hand of just 6d!

My investigations into the significance of the Tent brought into lively perspective the recorded activities of the Gigha Session.[8] The implications behind these apparently casual accounts transport us to a Gigha seething with Ministers, Elders and members of their congregations who travelled across Gigha Sound for the " Sacramental Week-end." All the details of the *Statistical Account,* all the profanities and calumnies, the " Poors " and the Elders, these all burgeon into life as we join the bustling throng. Let me tell you about it and you'll see what I mean.

The date of this annual event was always set by the Session for the beginning of May. In fact that is the one resolution that persists throughout the Record Book. What is not minuted, presumably it is one of those matters which is omitted because everyone knew about it, is the actual procedure. The month or so before the Thursday of the Sacramental Week-end was an extremely busy one for the Minister and the Elders whose duty it was to go round the Parish in the several districts to try to patch up any disagreements, to question people to make sure they knew their Faith, that is that they could say the Lord's Prayer and the Creed and had a reasonable knowledge of the Bible. In other words that they were in a fit state to receive Communion. At least that was the theory but the thoroughness of this examination depended very much on the Minister.

Anyhow, once the minister had assured himself of a person's worthiness he (or the Elder conducting the inquiry) gave him a Communion Token without which nobody would be admitted to the Sunday Service. The idea underlying this was that an unworthy communicant would defile the Communion for everyone else and to be debarred from the Sunday Service was a deep disgrace — socially as well as morally.

During this preparation time the " Linen " had to be got ready, the Elements fetched and the Tent made. The said Elements, the Bread and the Wine, would require a cart from Campbeltown and a special run of the Ferry because, believe it or not, during that particular week-end the population of the Parish of Gigha and Cara could be trebled with visiting ministers from other parishes together with hundreds of their various congregations! Many loaves of bread, and numerous bottles of wine would be needed.

And the Tent had to be erected. Obviously such a congregation could not fit into Gigha's little Church at Ardminish so a small shelter, exactly like a Sentry-box, would be built under which the minister giving any of the addresses or sermons could stand with his Bible. In fact the Tent was a shelter for the Holy Book, rather than the minister! In addition, if properly built, it would act rather like a sounding box by which the minister's voice would be projected to his enormous audience. Often the tent was placed at the foot of a slope while the congregation sat on the sides of a hill facing it. I don't know actually where Gigha's Tent was placed but certainly an ideal site would be down below the old Church (opposite the Hotel) while the people would sit on the slopes near the Church.

On the Thursday the people began to arrive and gather near the Church. Officially it was a Fast Day but this meant that like Sunday nobody did any unnecessary work, fasting did not necessarily apply to food. It was a joyful day when friends and relatives, men, women and children landed on Gigha from all over Kintyre and often from further afield. On the Friday, besides frequent sermons from the Tent, debates and discussions took place between the " Men," that is the more learned men of the congregations who often gave a lecture in Church on Sundays in addition to the Minister's sermon.

By Saturday the week-end was in full swing. Mr. Ross describes the scene:[9] On Saturday there is more Tent preaching, culminating in a great 'preparation Service.' By now most of the visitors have arrived and all about, can be seen people reading their Bibles or engaged in earnest prayer. Others indulge in less godly pursuits. Some never stray from the Ale House; young men and women wearing their best finery walk about for mutual admiration; and among them all hawkers, sturdy beggars and gangs of travelling tinkers are at work." Mr. Ross goes on to point out that, in spite of the somewhat mixed atmosphere, " many devout and simple saints found in these Communions, a true and intensely joyful trysting with their Saviour at his Table."

Everyone was out and about early on the Sunday itself, the Day of the Great Work. In the Church itself a long table covered with a linen cloth was erected along the length of the aisle. Round it stood a wooden fence, the Trivis. The Minister of the Parish, or another minister stood, at the opening to allow in only those who had either a token or a certificate from their own minister to say they could be admitted. Visitors would have secured their " Certificates " before leaving home. Without such a certificate any man or woman would be an " outsider " in any Scottish community where he or she was living or visiting.

People entered the Church in a quiet and orderly fashion, presenting their tokens or certificates. When the Table was full the Service began. Those left outside either read their Bibles or listened to sermons from the Tent. When the first sitting, so to speak was over, the communicants came out to sit on the grass or seek refreshment. Their places in Church were taken by others. Each Service was conducted by a different minister, and so it went on till everyone had taken Communion — a process that might last all day. Continuous sermons were preached for those outside.

Again I have no direct evidence of the next proceeding ever happening on Gigha but I am assured it would. On the Monday everyone reassembled once more in front of the Tent when the Minister of the Parish gave the Perlicue — the *Parle-queue* i.e. the Tail Speech, in which he gave a summary of the sermons to which the people had listened over the week-end. One by one he rehearsed what the Killean Minister had said, what the Tarbert minister and so on. After the Blessing everyone dispersed, visitors re-entered their boats and went home while the people of Gigha returned to Leim, Kinerarach, Ardlammy and the rest.

In due course they, in their turn, would journey across the Sound to visit Mainland Week-ends but, for the people of Gigha and Cara their own Sacramental Week-end was over for another year. On the Tuesday a new year would begin, a year during which, encouraged by the joyful reunions of the week-end and fortified by their Devotions they could, at least in theory, turn over to a clean page and face with cheerfulness and courage the new year that was beginning in the Parish of Gigha and Cara.

Modern Church

Chapter 7—The Nineteenth Century
The shape of things to come

As we journey on into the Nineteenth Century on Gigha the light is bright and the fog has almost dispersed. Our challenge henceforward is the interpretation of the knowledge we have. To change the metaphor, all this time we have been sailing down Loch Tarbert towards the Island. From a long way off all we could see was a humpy shape away in the distance. As we drew nearer some familiar landmarks stood out. Ploughing through the deep water of Gigha Sound, soon we could pick out the white farms, Tarbert, Drumeonbeg, then the Hotel, Ardminish and Gigulum until we reached the Pier. In our last couple of chapters we actually landed on the Island but now we can really walk about and investigate it thoroughly, so that, as the nineteenth Century progresses, gradually we can watch a recognisable Gigha taking shape before our eyes.

When the Reverend James Curdie came to write his Account of the state of his Parish in the 1840's, although he did not comment at such length as his predecessor, he did record some very illuminating facts.[1] Generally speaking I get the impression that life on Gigha had not changed all that much during the first few years of the 19th Century. The Church was in a satisfactory state even if the floor was below the level of the damp. He seems to have been perfectly happy in his Manse which he noted had been built in 1818 and repaired in 1828. So that, for the moment at least, is one satisfactory conclusion to a disturbed story.

After confirming what we already know that " the landowners of the Island are Captain Alexander McNeill and the Lady of the Hon. A. H. Morton and Miss MacDonald Lockhart of Lee and Carnwath " he went on to write " There are two Mansion Houses on the Island used only occasionally by the late proprietors but are now occupied by tenants."

Of the two mansion houses whose lairds were non-resident one was probably Achamore House in which in 1841 a Mrs. Platt lived about whom we know nothing. The date on the front of the present house suggests that it was built in 1884 and we shall follow up the exciting adventures of that house later.

The traditional second Mansion, that of Galloichille, is the cottage down at Galloichille now occupied by John and Lily Martin. Certainly, although much altered over the years, the skeleton of the house, with a high large Hall does bear this out and in any case I have learnt too much respect for popular tradition to dismiss the suggestion completely.

In the back of my mind lies another possibility. In the mid-Seventeenth Century the Great House of Gigha was down near Leim, according to a map published by the contemporary Dutch firm of Bleau.[2] The Reverend Timothy Pont, the renowned cartographer, placed there the most important house on the Island, a fact denoted by its possession of two large towering chimneys. One day recently Mr. Bicket, the present tenant of Leim Farm, showed me, a few hundred yards North East of his steading, the ruined walls and foundations of a large irregular rectangular house some sixty feet long and running over forty feet back towards a wooded cliff, forming an ideal position both from the point of view of defence and of amenity. On the rough grassy floor it was just possible to see what may well have been dividing walls of rooms.

Still another Great House existed on Gigha on Bleau's map. At the North End stood Balmoir, distinguished from Leim by the possession of only one chimney and two open stacks. This house appears from its ruins, which you can see today beyond Kinerarach, to have been smaller than Leim but in the one reasonably complete gable wall is a rather lovely long narrow window, certainly not the window of an ordinary house on Gigha in the seventeenth Century.

Balmoir brings to my mind in the firm Gigha tradition that, at one time, "long ago," Gigha was divided between two families. Some doubt exists as to which family lived at the South End, although the Graham family has been suggested, but legend is quite clear that the North End, beyond what is locally known as " The Great Gate " (the Druid Stone area) was ruled by the Galbraiths. From the Nineteenth Century Census Returns, it is perfectly true that the farms at the North End were all held by Galbraiths and it is noticeable that the few Grahams living on the Island then were down in the South. Furthermore the Galbraiths, with one exception, were farmers while the Grahams were Fishermen: the two traditional occupations of Gigha people.

Whatever the truth of the details of this firm local tradition, the moral for us is that when we are trying to sort out the quarrels of the McNeills and McLeans, the MacDonalds and Campbells about the ' overlordship ' of Gigha we must always remember that these give us little clue about the actual life being lived on the Island. As we found when reading the Session Minutes, beneath the seemingly calm waters of the Sound of Gigha lie hidden tides and currents which we can perceive only on the rare occasions when we catch a fleeting glimpse beneath the surface.

One of Mr. Curdie's remarks provides us with a key to the development of life on Gigha in the 19th Century: " Between Gigulum and Gigha there is a Sound which affords good anchorage for large vessels, and is frequented by Her Majesty's cutters and by vessels going to and from England and Ireland — there is a ferry from each of the properties to Tayinloan on the Mainland." Then he made the most important statement of all. " A Steamer which plies between West Loch Tarbert and Islay passes the North End of Gigha thrice a week in the summer and once a week in winter and a boat attends for the purpose of landing passengers." The Age of Steam had arrived, even on Gigha!

Following the *Comet* of 1812 a multitude of steamers began to sail practically everywhere, including Islay and therefore probably Gigha.[3] In 1826 the Pier at West Loch Tarbert was built and a vessel called the *Maid of Islay* sailed from there to Port Askaig on Tuesdays. By 1846 a paddler called the *Modern Athens* had replaced her and sailed from Glasgow on Mondays for Port Ellen and made two trips to the West Loch before setting off for Glasgow again on Fridays. In 1849 the *Islay* did this run but the *Modern Athens* may well have maintained the West Loch Tarbert — Islay run itself.

The first steamer we definitely know about which called at Gigha was MacBrayne's *Lochiel* in 1877. By 1878 she had been succeeded by the *Glencoe* who remained on the run till the paddler *Pioneer* started in 1905. The Pier was not built till 1895 so before that intending passengers had to embark or disembark into a rowing boat out from the shore in order to travel by the said steamer.[4] When Mr. Curdie wrote he commented that two ferrymen operated from the Island, one from each estate. As he noted each would convey passengers from and to the Mainland, one based at Galloichille, one at Achnaha. After the Galloichille estate was absorbed into the main estate in 1865 the Ferryman's duties were to meet the Steamer at whichever End it was calling. Even a glance at the *Glencoe's* timetable makes me feel that the Ferryman must have had his wits about him to know just where he would have to have his boat!

We'll return to Achnaha in a minute but meantime let's consider the Steamer Ferryman. In the Census Returns of 1841 living at Galleyport was James Fletcher, Ferryman. James was getting on in life and by 1861 he had been succeeded by his son Malcolm. Meanwhile a fisherman named William Orr had moved from Ardminish where he was living in 1841 to the other cottage at Galloichille — the cottage in fact which had been noted as belonging to the " Spirit Dealer " or " Inn Charge Keeper " of Galloichille but which became vacant when the Island became one. By 1861 Willie, still a fisherman officially, was married to Ellen MacMillan whose father was tenant of North Drumachro and they had three little sons, Alan, Alexander and James.

I suspect that William was acting as assistant ferryman even then because in 1871 he had become official ferryman, a post he held till the Pier was built. In fact Willie Orr, the Ferryman, is one of the renowned characters of Gigha. Also famous was the beauty of his wife Ellie. Now I knew that their grandson Angus McNeill son of their daughter, another Ellie,[5] is the present tenant of Kinerarach (1978) so off I went to see him. He showed me what must be one of the greatest treasures of Gigha, an oil painting dated 1880 showing Willie's open wooden boat, with huge heavy oars, struggling through foam-crested waves. The dozen or so passengers are wind-blown and wet, huddling against each other, either because of the tossing of the boat or in order to find some kind of shelter. I wonder if they still faced the horrifying prospect of climbing on to the *Glencoe* or the equally daunting scramble on to the seaweed-covered rocks of Gigha!

The Achnaha Ferry goes back as far as we have records. In the Kirk Session Records Donald McQuilken was the Ferryman. He was succeeded by his son Malcolm and in 1841 Donald MacDonald was at the Ferryhouse. By 1851 Archibald McNeill had taken over the job which he held till his death in 1885. By the way he has no known connection with the McNeills of today.

A resident on the Island has lent me a priceless document dated October 1885 which confirms W. J. Scarlett's appointment of John Wotherspoon as Ferryman. The conditions of his tenure are set out above the list of fares he is allowed to charge. John's remuneration consisted of the Ferry Croft " except that piece surrounding the house of Mrs. McNeill which she rents " and he may have all the " Ferry Dues." These are set out in detail:— one passenger 2/- and where more than 6 passengers 6d. each passenger; one horse 4/-; every additional horse 2/-; one cow 2/-, every additional cow 1/-; sheep per head 3d.; one pig 2/-, if more than 4 pigs each 4d; bulls and stallions double fare; 2 one-year-old stirks to be considered equal to one cow; barley 6d. per quarter; telegram 2/-.

For this John Wotherspoon had to convey free " the proprietor and his family, friends and servants " as well as " such tradesmen and others that may be employed on the Proprietor's affairs." He had always to be ready, if wanted, to do work about the estate, always being allowed time to work his own croft. If he himself went further away than Tayinloan he had to provide a substitute ferryman at his own expense. In addition to the Ferry he was responsible for " such boats as Colonel Scarlett may happen to have on Gigha at any one time, whether for fishing or any other purpose. John could be dismissed at the Proprietor's pleasure but he himself had to give one month's notice. John remained the Ferryman at Achnaha till the outbreak of the First War when Archibald McCougan took over.

No doubt at all exists, then, that the people of Gigha during the greater part of the 19th century had ready means of access to the labour-hungry Mainland and the Clyde Estuary, the mills of Paisley and either from Gigha or from the Clyde plenty of opportunities existed to venture even further afield to the welcoming outposts of the Empire.

Mr. Curdie remarked, strangely enough, that " very few have emigrated from Gigha to a foreign country " but, he went on " the young men and women leave home for service at an early period and are absent in many instances for years and generally for half a year." At least two thirds of the young people will always leave any but the larger industrial complexes to seek work so Gigha is not strange in this respect. In his fascinating book " The Crofting Community " James Hunter remarks that some farms on Skye were understocked with animals but overstocked with people.[6] This situation would indeed be less desirable than young people leaving home to seek good jobs.

If you study the Population Returns you will find that the decrease over the years is partly accounted for by more than just young people leaving.[7] In fact every thirty years or so, in each generation, groups of perhaps four or five families left the Island. The reasons for this are not far to seek. The mid-century was an uncertain time on the Island what between the long-drawn out bankruptcy proceedings and the untimely death of Alexander McNeill in 1850. Added to this we find evidence of enticements to emigrate. We must never forget Neil and Grisella who, almost certainly, remained in touch with Gigha people who in their turn went out to find a more promising life, braving the terrible conditions of the emigrant ships.

Evidence exists of publicity agents coming over to Scotland from developing countries to encourage would-be emigrants. Hunter cites a " posse of recruiting agents from the Canadian Fencible regiment which visited the Highlands and Islands in 1804." Volunteers and their families were offered free passages to Canada and promised that land would be made available to them on their discharge. Although the Campbeltown records show lists of families who left Kintyre on emigrant ships so far I have not definitely identified any from Gigha but I feel at least some families would take advantage of boarding a ship leaving from Kintyre.

Bearing all this in mind, we must not forget Mr. Curdie's remark that " not much emigration had recently taken place to foreign parts " and remind ourselves that all this time ship-building and industry generally were booming on the Mainland, which, after all was much more accessible. Gigha men would be welcome in the shipyards, in the merchant ships and the Cotton Industry of Paisley and the surrounding districts. These and their many ancillary jobs would appear very enticing to the people of Ardailly and Ardachy, Kinerarach and the other settlements.

All this seems quite reasonable and straightforward but our strangest task is to look more closely at the dramatic drop in the population around the 50's and 60's. Popular legend on Gigha centre this around the strange and sudden decline of the numbers of the once flourishing Galbraith family who seem to have almost disappeared from the Island. It is certainly true that in 1841 Galbraiths with large families rented Tarbert, North Ardminish, Highfield, Ardailly, Drumeonbeg and North Drumachro. By 1851 they had left North Drumachro and by 1871 all but Drumeonbeg were held by other tenants. If we look at numbers we find that some 50 lived on Gigha in 1851. Some eighteen died before 1871 but this does not account for the fact that in that year only 19 were left of whom 12 were over 60 years of age. Detailed examination shows that the decline was largely due to the departure of youngish parents and their young families.

The fact that families of McNeills still live on Gigha today has overlaid the undoubted fact that almost as many McNeills left in the exodus as Galbraiths. The McNeills tended to be fisherfolk, the Galbraiths farmers. Of forty-five McNeills on the Island in 1841, 29 were still there in 1851 but by 1871 only nineteen remained of which the younger ones accounted for only nineteen and ten of those of one related family. From these ten the McNeills of Gigha today are descended.

Another point: on Gigha today almost everyone will tell you that one day last century (date unspecified) a group of thirteen (or fifteen) families left the North End to emigrate, (destination unknown). As I have said already local legend is ignored at one's peril so one day I added up the number of families who appear to have left Gigha around the 50's and 60's only to find that between 1851 and '61 eleven or twelve separate groups who lived all over the Island did indeed leave but whether they left together or, in fact from the North End I do not know.

The question that arises is whether or not this could be regarded as a " Clearance " by which Social Historians mean an instance of men and women being forced, often with great cruelty, to leave their homes as happened on other Islands and in the Highlands. So great was the concern over this that a Royal Commission was appointed in 1865 to report on it.[8] In none of their bulky reports do I find Gigha mentioned. Moreover none of these farms, with the possible exception of Kinerarach, was left untenanted. Very little evidence, if any, exists that an attempt was made to make large enclosures for sheep rearing and in any case who, in the 50's and 60's, would do so? Mr. Curdie recorded that Alexander McNeill made, at his own expense, a new road to the Mill and had the Mill Loch drained for peat so it doesn't seem likely that he was going in for expensive sheep rearing leading to the misery of clearances. By the time the Scarletts came in the 1860's the process of emigration was well under way. In fact when we come to look at some of the places which were deserted we will find that almost certainly people had been leaving for many years before the 1850's. Finally I doubt if sheep rearing, limited in scope as it would be, would be rewarding enough for any landowner to attempt any large scale clearance.

As I say, we find at Kinerarach that some confusion exists. According to the Valuation Rolls for the latter half of the century one Allan Pollock was the tenant and occupier and yet his name appears nowhere at all in the Census Returns which record, at Kinerarach three cottages, one of which is our friend Willie Orr's, one is a Shepherd's and the other a Farm Labourer. By the end of the century all this has gone and Kinerarach was an ordinary tenanted farm. In the 70's Ardlammy was said to be " under a Manager for the Proprietors " but whether this was an attempt to make it a Home Farm or a sheep farm is not clear. Like

84

Kinerarach it reverted to being a tenanted farm at the end of the century.

Sometimes I wonder if on Gigha we find the opposite of clearances! The uncertainties at home and the encouragements from abroad tempted so many people to depart that lairds and farmers alike had to adjust their policies to a less well-populated Island.

So much then for what one might term the more dramatic side of Gigha life in the 19th Century. If the Island was to prosper then some folk must think it worth while to stay, conditions must make them resist the temptation to leave but, above all new families would have to be attracted to come to infuse fresh blood so that together new and old could build a happy and healthy successful economy.

To find out about work conditions we turn again to Mr. Curdie who reported that Fishing continued " Cod and Ling and large Haddocks as well as Mackerel, Lythe and Cuddies which abound near the coast." Of the farms he said " most of them are on leases of seven to fifteen years' duration which is a distinct improvement." He also said that Captain McNeill had recently built " two good farm houses and several good farm-offices."

Detailed examination of the Census Returns show that as the 19th Century advanced certain groups of cottages became established, some old clachans disappear but in most cases in each clachan one building was developed as a farm-house with a few cottages attached. By the end of the century the groups of cottages remain while the Farm-plus-Cottages have coalesced into Farm-Steads.

On the subject of the groups of cottages Mr. Curdie stated that " no village exists on the Island " which is strange because he wrote for publication in 1845, while the Census Returns of 1841 show that in the latter year fifty-eight people lived in Ardminish Village in fourteen houses. This, you will remember, is the exact number which John McNeill built at the end of the 18th Century. In 1861 another five cottages were recorded and, significantly enough, in one of them lived as "lodgers" three masons, two from Campbeltown and one from Killean. Further to this, Neil Bannatyne, who today lives at Carnvickoye, showed me a stone clearly marked 1856 which he found, when demolishing old cottages a few years ago to build the present ones. He told me it was on one of the more Southerly houses which were " newer " than the others so we can say with reasonable certainty that Ardminish Village was built in the late Eighteenth Century and extended in the mid-Nineteenth.

As to the other hamlets: Keill changed its spelling, (Kile, Keills and Keill) but otherwise it stood much as it does today. New Quay was called New Cottages in 1841 but thereafter New Quay Cottages. The Drumeonbeg crofts soldiered on, sometimes one house was divided into two but again fishermen and farmworkers lived in them much as they seem to have done for some time. The group at Gigulum do not appear in the census until the 1890's.

If you look at the map you'll see that Keill Cottages are on the spine of the Island but Ardminish, New Quay and Gigulum are on the *East*. It was the groups on the *West* which suffered most from the departure of so many people from the Island.

Of the vanished homes of Gigha probably the most dramatic ruination was Ardailly, away over by the Mill. I am almost certain we are just too late to see it in its hey-day because even by 1841 two places were listed; North Ardailly with a farm and two cottages but yet, the day I was over there with Mr. and Mrs. McNeill Kivett,[9] we counted the ruins of at least twelve or thirteen stone houses although many were so ruinous it was difficult to be certain about numbers.

The lost village of Gigha which has always intrigued me is Ardachy (pronounced Artaky with the accent on the first syllable!) so one day I persuaded Betty to show me exactly where it lies as I have never managed to find it away out on the wild west coast. We started off down the Ardlammy road. The bracken which, when the two of us were cairn-hunting in the Spring was curling in fresh green fronds, was now brown and crackling. Brambles hung in lush black bushes where we had seen whitish pink blossom. The golden flag irises marking the springs had gone leaving forests of bright green spear-like leaves. Clumps of deep purple Ling and lighter Bell heather and blue Harebells grew among the grassy tussocks.

Betty indicated a path going East up the ridge. " Have you been up to *Croc nan Ordag?* It's just up there." Indeed I had. One day in the summer Jeanette Blackwood of Ardlammy had taken me up to that roofless ruin of a cottage which had in the mid-19th Century housed three families but is now almost totally overgrown. I shall never forget sitting up there in the sunshine listening to one of Gigha's youngest residents telling me one of the oldest of Gigha's legends. " Once long ago, a long time ago, two families on Gigha met here to have a fight. The victors cut off their enemies' thumbs and buried the thumbs here. That's why it's called the Hill of Thumbs. Cunning wasn't it? After all they couldn't do much fishing or farming without their thumbs could they?"

As I was remembering this Betty had wended her way further along towards the North West. She pointed up again to the hill on our right. " That's the way up to the Glen where one of my own ancestors, Angus of the Glen, lived. There's no good going there. It's all overgrown." In fact in the mid-19th century no fewer than three cottages had stood there where now even the walls have all but disappeared.

By now we stood above the chasm at the bottom of which lies *Tar an Tarb*, the Loch of the Bull, where in the black water a swan and her cygnets swam gracefully where once the last distiller of Gigha cast his equipment on the approach of the Excise man. Away to the North, high up, Keefi's eyrie looked out over the approaches to Gigha.

Slowly but surely Betty struck over to the left through a remote and lonely wilderness. Far off we could just hear the splash of the waves against the western rocks. Three dark birds flew overhead the swish of their regularly beating wings soughing in the wind. " Mergansers," commented Betty. " They roost at Rhunahaorine in hundreds on the rocks. I'll take you out there for a picnic next Summer."

At the summit of a little hill she stopped. "That's Ardachy down there!" Below lay a deep oval bowl of green and rocky land. Down into that eerie lost world we slithered. Just over a hundred years ago eleven people had lived here in three cottages but the numerous foundations, as at Ardailly, told of far more houses having been here long before that. This settlement had become deserted over a period of years but I doubt if we'll we'll ever know when or where the people went. Some living near Ardailly may well have followed Neil and Grisella but many may well simply have moved across to one of the cottages on the more promising East. Certainly once the West road began to fall into decay the folk of Ardachy must have found life very difficult.[10] No arable land lay near, the sea was a long way off and, even at that was the stormiest and rockiest bit of the coast. Without the earlier Census Returns we shall probably never solve the mystery. All I do know is that John MacMillan, of the old Gigha MacMillans who were once at Leim and Drumachro, once showed me his father Hector's birth Certificate dated 1860 which recorded that Hector was born at Ardachy. When Hector was a baby his parents moved to Ardminish Village where Johnnie still lives, as we shall find out when we visit this man, one of the last of the 'old' fishermen of Gigha.

While I was sitting on the doorstep of what had once been a house thinking about all this Betty was squelching about over on the West side where there seemed to me more greenery than anywhere else. "Come and look! Whatever else Ardachy had or hadn't got it had the best spring on Gigha. In the winter it must have been nearly a pond." Sure enough the bright green iris spikes spread over an area of four or five yards under which the mud was sodden, even at this time when most of the rest of the land was dry.

As we walked back past Ardlammy fields Mr. Blackwood was taking advantage of that same dry weather to take his Combine over the field of corn to get the harvest home. However tempting it is to dwell on the mystery of Ardachy our road ahead lies with the harvests and the farms of Gigha because the key to the future of Gigha was to lie with the farms. Were they going to hold out sufficient evidence of prosperity to entice new tenants and labourers to come to take the place of those who were going away?

Once more Mr. Curdie gives us a clue, two clues in fact. " Most of the farms," he reported " are now on leases of seven to fifteen years' duration which is a distinct improvement " and again, when he was discussing the changes that Alexander McNeill had undertaken, he included the " building of two good slated farmhouses and several good slated farm offices." The minister certainly put his finger right on the crucial point.

The Census Returns tell the ongoing story of the evolution of the Clachans. Still, in 1841 at Tarbert and Carnvickoye (spelt Caruamhiceam dhu!) two cottages stood beside a large house wherein lived about a dozen men and women of different ages and occupations but by 1851 only a farmer and his family lived in the main house and the last wraith of the old clachan had disappeared. Achavenish, Drumeonbeg and Drumeonmore did not appear to have any cottages by 1841 but Leim, Drumachro, North and South, North Ardminish and Highfield all had three or four until the 1860's. With the exception of Ardlammy which had one cottage and Highfield with three none of these had cottages by the 1890's.

We have already discussed the curious case of Kinerarach when we were thinking about clearances so now we can take up the subject of the most teasing farm of all: Achamore. Tracing its progress I follow Anderson and discuss the decay of the old Chanterrioch.[11] Chanterrioch was mentioned in the oldest documents but never in the Session Records nor yet in the 1797 Sasine while the name Achamore appeared officially for the first time in the 1836 Bankruptcy Proceedings. Achamore was, you remember, where John McNeill's ' store ' was – *not* you'll notice his *clachan* or farm. John, too, was experimenting somewhere with growing hay for winter feed. To appear to confuse us still further Lachlan MacLachlan was put in charge of " Shensrioch where he lives and also Leim." So we find, at more or less the same place on Gigha three names of clachan/farms Chanterrioch – Achamore – Shensrioch.

As a start we find that the Gaelic pronunciation of Shensrioch approximates to Chanterrioch so I think we can take it these are two terms for the same place. Looking at the map we find it is away out on the West coast on the present Achamore land. Seeking clues in the Census Returns we find that, in 1841, Achamore was an established farm with four cottages and next to it lay a separate establishment called Shensrioch which consisted of a cottage with one family and a large house in which lived a number of people of both sexes, various ages and a selection of occupations. Twenty years later it had disappeared completely from the Returns.

I don't know if you will agree with me but I think that strictly speaking John McNeill's nearest clachan when he came to live at Achamore in the " old manse " would be Shensrioch, the old Chanterrioch on the coast. That would be a most unsuitable situation for a Laird to have a successful experimental farm in the neighbourhood of the house he was establishing at Achamore. All the evidence points to John setting up his farm in a more favourable situation more central to the available arable land, a decision which led to the run-down and final disappearance of the old Chanterrioch/Shensrioch which was the only known clachan besides Ardachy which faded away without leaving a modern farm. You will notice that in neither case was there any extent of good arable land available in the immediate vicinity.

So intrigued was I with this strange problem that I went off up to Achamore to see if the present tenant, John MacDonald knew of any remains of a village on his land. John greeted me with his usual welcoming grin. " It'll be Hill Top Town you'll be looking for," he said. " Hop in the Land Rover and I'll take you over!" Accompanied by two-and-a-half year old Malcolm, a stalwart young man who looks set to be the third generation of his family to farm Achamore, we went South towards Leim, pausing a moment to look at the Bodach and Caillaich standing impassive on their hill. In front of us lay a wide cultivated field. " This is where my father and I cleared away the Golf Course. That large heap of stones in the middle must have been cottages but I don't think there would be many." He drove westwards, stopped beside a largish expanse of rocks covered with scrubby bushes. We walked round it, trying to clear away some of the tough grass. The flat stone of a doorstep appeared, then large stones which disappeared into the bushes in very much the way a wall would have done. John meanwhile found some more among the undergrowth. " I must come and clear this lot properly some day," he said looking at the wide area of bushes.

Perhaps we'll persuade an expert Archaeologist to come to look when he does because I just couldn't even guess the age of the buildings. I agree that the place occupies the same place on the map as Chanterrioch/Shensrioch but the whole set-up of the stones I saw was remarkably reminiscent of both *Dun Trinsse* and *Dun Chibhich* as the Kintyre Book notes (no. 164) " the outer face of the fort wall is carried right across it, forming a step or threshold at the mouth of the entrance passage."

Since Anderson explored Hill Top Town some forty years ago much has changed of the series of " benches " he spoke of which are not now obvious. I think we were rooting about that day at what he called ' the rock Citadel ' (p. 127) as the rocky rough hill would be just about the 85 by 35 feet he mentions. When he visited Ardachy I suggested an excavation there would be of value but I almost think that such a dig at Hill Top Town/ Shensrioch/Chanterrioch might not tell us even more about the past centuries of Gigha's History.

As we returned to Achamore it crossed my mind that John McNeill may well have been right in changing the location into the centre of more arable land. As we stood once more in the old steading John MacDonald told me how he had discovered the timber skeletons of cottages incorporated into the stables and byres when he had been modernising the Farm for his Milking Parlour. In fact the same is true of both Ardlammy and Leim; proof of what happened to the old farm plus cottages complexes when the farmsteads were built

Only a few ' extra ' houses were actually built, as far as we know, during the 19th Century. In 1884 Achamore House itself was either built or re-built as the date in front proclaims but I ask you to be patient till we have an opportunity of entering the house which, by that time, will have had an exciting adventure leading to extensive re-building. Perhaps this is the place to confess that one of my chief difficulties in writing out the history of Gigha has been the order in which to lay it before you. I must resist the temptation just to pour out all the information as if emptying a treasure chest from the sea!!

One intriguing establishment was built at Woodside where the second Mr. Scarlett built a " House for a Gamekeeper and Kennels." Here he kept a pack of hounds, not for fox hunting as no foxes live on Gigha and in any case the terrain would be quite unsuitable for fox-hunters. Mr. Scarlett used his hounds for hunting hares. I have not actually investigated myself but Duncan McSporran, who has lived all his life on Gigha tells me, you can walk on paths and trails all over the Island using the gates specially constructed so that the first rider could flick off the latch with his whip while the last could likewise shut it — both without dismounting!

Now we come to what, to me, is the crucial point of this whole chapter namely the numbers and calibre of those who did not leave the Island on the emigrant ships, and the entrance into Gigha of vitalising new families and the extent to which these groups integrated to form the basis of a new society and economy, beneficial to all concerned.

Taking first those who remained on Gigha we find that the family with the longest tenancy of one farm were the McCougans who remained in South Drumachro from the time it ceased to be the Manse in 1818 till early in the 1920's. Long tenancies too were held by the Macallums at Ardlammy and the Smiths at Carnvickoye but, so far as I know none of them remains on Gigha today. McMillans lived almost all the century at Leim, North Drumachro and the Smiddy but the same Christian names of Alexander, Hector and John occur so often that it is difficult to tell from which of them, if any, Alexander of Ardachy was descended who is the grandfather of our present representative of the family, John McMillan.

Also remaining on the Island to render faithful service were descendants of John MacDonald, Archibald Henderson, James Wotherspoon, Duncan McVean, William Orr and Angus

McNeill, all of whom are recorded as living and working on Gigha before the middle of last century. Each one is still represented today. Grahams and Galbraiths, the two legendary families have of course resident descendants, all of them through the female line. Finally Donald McQuilken, the Ferryman of the Session Records had a son called Sweyn who is represented by a female descendant who lives at Ardminish.

Now, to the newcomers – those who came into Gigha to fill the vacancies left by the various emigrants. Of course several families, farmers taking up seven or fifteen year leases, made their contribution to the economy but, here we are concerned with the people who integrated with the existing inhabitants to help directly to build the Gigha of today.

The first to arrive, as far as I can find, were the McSporran family, who arrived at Achamore between 1851 and 1861, and altered the farm considerably, for a time.[13] In the farm itself lived Dugald McSporran and with his mother and four of his elder brothers who acted as his ploughmen and labourers! The cottages disappeared, almost certainly to provide adequate accommodation for another of Dugald's older brothers, Malcolm, who was married to a lady called Janet Montgomery, an Ayrshire girl and they had a son William who was four when they appear in 1861 as well as two other children. Eventually their large family also included Mary and Duncan. Thirty years later Malcolm and Janet still lived at Achamore, Dugald and the other brothers were dead, the cottages had reappeared and Malcolm and his family lived in the farmhouse. This situation obtained till the very end of the century when Malcolm died and Achamore changed its name and function once more.

Before the last quarter of the Century other people appear in the records who were to exert a lasting influence. Men like Robert Cavana came to live in one of Achamore's cottages as a gardener, Angus Wilkieson who worked at North Drumachro, George Allen who rented a cottage up at Achamore, Neil Bannatyne who came from Kintyre to succeed the MacMillans in the Smiddy and, Alexander MacPherson who took over the Hotel before the end of the century.

This brings us to the final and the most important point of our discussion about the population of Gigha: the degree of integration between the new families so that the future of the Island would not be jeopardised by a population weakened by constant remarrying. Naturally we do find, during the last quarter of the 19th Century a certain number of marriages between older families. Angus McNeill married Ellie Orr, Duncan Henderson married Flora MacDonald, Hugh Wotherspoon married one of the last of the Galbraiths, while Donald MacDonald married Isobel McNeill.

Of the many alliances between new and old one important series for the future resulted from the marriage between Angus Wilkieson and Margaret Galbraith of Drumeonbeg. In due course their elder son married Katie MacPherson, daughter of the hotel keeper, their daughter Phemie married George Allen while their second son, Angus, chose his bride from the Mainland.

Probably the most extensive and influencial series of marriages concerned the McSporran family of Achamore. Do you remember that little four year old boy William? When he grew up he married Catherine Graham so, as the Angus Wilkieson/Margaret Galbraith marriage knit the Galbraiths into the new weave of Gigha this marriage kept the Graham blood in the population. Not only that but their son Malcolm married in turn another of the Graham family, Sarah, while daughter Susan married Neil Orr, a son of Willie the Ferryman. To complete the alliance of old and new Mary, one of Malcolm and Janet McSporran's daughters married Duncan McNeill, a son of Angus of the Glen. All these marriages have descendants living on Gigha today, playing an active part in its flourishing life. You will meet many of them as we journey on through the twentieth Century. You've already met one, our old friend Betty McNeill one of the granddaughters of that marriage between Mary McSporran and Duncan McNeill.

As time has gone on, of course the distinction between new and old has been erased not only by more intermarriage in the next generation but also by many marriages with people from the Mainland so that the population ferment of the 19th Century which we have been watching has, in the end, resulted in nothing but good for the Island.

Isn't it curious how, when we look back over the long way we have come since the days of John McNeill and the Session Records how fortune seems to have run smoothly for the Islanders? To work out how far this was due to their Geographical position, the good harbourage, the fertility of Gigha soil whether for grain or potatoes and how far it was due to any human agency is indeed difficult. Yet natural advantages by themselves are never enough, they have to be seized and utilised if their full benefit is to be reaped.

All this is very true but I shouldn't like to suggest you consider whether the really lucky day for Gigha was when John McNeill bought the Island way back at the end of the 18th Century. It was he who deliberately turned the face of the Island Eastwards; he made up the Eastern road, he built a school on the East and a substantial house for the Inn Chargekeeper as well as the village of Ardminish. We have seen that he had an interest in the Island in the mid-century so he may very well have been instrumental in repairing the Church in 1780, he certainly played a leading part in securing an efficient minister. Wherever the Mansion House had been before his time he set about establishing the Laird's headquarters in the centre of the more potentially prosperous part of the Island where too he almost certainly built up his main farm where he began to experiment with better methods of farming. Would I be wrong in suggesting that John McNeill, like King Haco of Norway many centuries before realised the importance of Gigha's sandy bays and creeks which made good harbours and which were situated on the East of the Island?

Whatever the truth of all that the joyful fact remains that now we press on with our story to live at a time when under the intelligent leadership of a new Laird, the third Scarlett, the people of Gigha entered into the fruits of the labours of the 19th Century.

KINTYRE FROM ARDMINISH, ISLE OF GIGHA

A 9734

Old Ardminish looking towards Kintyre with Tigh Rudh in background.

Chapter 8—The clear light of living memory

At last the time has come when we no longer need to reconstruct the life of the people of Gigha from deeds and documents. Now, as the 19th Century becomes the 20th, we have an abundance of contemporary evidence which dispels the fog so that we walk in the clear vitalising light of Gigha. Of course we still have a background of official papers but three priceless treasures brings them to life. An album of over fifty photographs taken around 1908 gives incontrovertible evidence of the appearance, not only of the houses and farms, but of the actual inhabitants.[1] In the second place, due to the generosity of Tom Gillies, who used to be at Tarbert Farm, we can glean precious treasure from a curious brochure compiled for a Sale of the Island in 1911; a Sale which, for some reason, never took place. Above all we can enjoy, and profit by, the youthful memories of those who now rank as Senior Citizens of Gigha. Faithfully stored in the mind for many years, the memory of youth shines with lively brilliance as these years increase. In the light of all these encouragements we set out with joyous expectancy on our journey through 20th Century Gigha.

William James Yorke Scarlett, who succeeded his father as Laird of the Island in 1893, early showed that he had grasped the essential fact that he and his tenants were partners: the Island would be a viable possession for himself and his family just so long as he created conditions which encouraged the co-operation of his tenants in increasing its overall prosperity.

The very first photograph in the Album provides us with a significant clue to his appreciation of the best way to set about achieving his objective; " *the Pioneer* approaching the Pier,"

The Pioneer approaching Gigha, 1908.

we read. In 1895 W. J. Yorke Scarlett declared that he had acquired "the right, title and interest which belonged to Queen Victoria over so much of all that piece of land being part of the foreshore and bed of the sea below high water mark situate at *Port na Carraigh* which is occupied by the pillars and supports of the pier thereon constructed by me for which permission was granted by the Board of Trade and registered in the General Register of Sasines, 1895." Building that solid wooden pier right out into deep water, at the most suitable place for such a pier, did away with the clumsy procedure of passengers and cargo being ferried ashore in Willie Orr's boat to be landed on a slippery jetty. In my opinion this was the one basic necessity if Gigha was to have a chance of success in the twentieth Century.

While Mr. Scarlett had no intention of being an absentee landlord his plans were so ambitious that he would require the services of an Estate Factor with both organising ability and the appropriate expertise to be his executive officer. With his usual attention to detail he built, for his Factor, The Lodge at the entrance to the newly made South Drive to Achamore House. The first factor, Mr. Douglas, left in 1898 to be succeeded by William Watt Philip, a member of an Aberdeenshire farming family, who had been trained as a forester at Balmoral and who took a deep interest in the breeding of Clydesdale horses which he regarded as the basis of successful arable farming.[2] As it turned out these were exactly the qualifications Mr. Scarlett required. One of the first things the new factor did was to build on to the North gable-end of the Lodge an Estate Office to be the centre of Estate business.

The Lodge and Estate Office, 1908.

The official power house of course was Mr. Scarlett's own residence up at Achamore which, during this period was known as the Mansion House. As we know, John McNeill had done some building there at the end of the 18th Century and, according to the date on the front of the House more building was added in 1884, but, a few years after Yorke Scarlett's succession a disastrous fire destroyed the top storey of the old House which was never re-built. In Achamore House a painting of the House before the fire still hangs. The fire happened one afternoon when the Family were off the Island and the servants had all gone over to Leim to play golf — incidentally one piece of evidence about the existence of that curious feature of the Island! Driving along the road in his trap, the local grocer and shoemaker, Sandy Orr, saw the flames and later immortalised his story in Gigha's famous ballad, *Flames at Achamore* which has been recited for me by Angus Allen of South Drumachro who heard Sandy himself recite it at many a Gigha gathering.

> *I lowsed the horse out o' the cart,*
> *I galloped to the Shore*
> *I cried out to the golfers*
> *" There's fire at Achamore!"*
>
> *I jumped into the passages*
> *So loudly did I roar*

> " There's flames at Achamore, boys,
> There's flames at Achamore."

The servants rushed back and managed to save much of the furniture while the Butler threw the silver out of the window The China, similarly ' saved ' by a zealous housemaid was not so fortunate.

How much of the House had to be rebuilt I do not know but, certainly, the photographs of it and indeed its appearance today show that the Mansion House since 1895 has indeed been as "picturesque and unique " as the 1911 Brochure claims. The spacious Entrance Hall and the upper landing, the wide stairs as well as many of the floors are oak while the carved banister is a thing of joy. Most of the walls of the downstairs rooms were pannelled in oak too, all of which must have been imported as very little grows on the Island even today.

The Mansion House, 1908.

The clear Gigha light streams in through skillfully carved mullion windows and deep wide sash windows. The pleasing shape of many of the rooms tells of the employment of an expert architect, as well as the expenditure of a good deal of money. The Drawing Room which, in these days had two large fire-places looked very gay and welcoming, Summer and Winter, with the handsome old Axminster carpet (still one of the treasures of the House), the Chinese wallpaper forming a background for the floral chintz-covered chairs.

Remember this House was no show piece, deserted for most of the year but a family home the scene of many parties, quiet days and merry evenings and a welcoming holiday house for family guests. Mrs. Katie Wilkieson, now in her ninety-second year who has lived all but the first three of them on Gigha remembers when she used to go to " help " in this lovely House:— " The Scarlett's," she told me, " lived quite a lot on Gigha, not just for holidays as some other lairds did in those days. In the House we had three housemaids, a cook and three maids in the Kitchen, three in the Laundry besides a Butler, two footmen, a Hall boy and, when they were needed, a children's nurse and nursemaids. Of course the ladies had their maids and the men their valets. They all, of course used the Cycle path to and from the House. You know, that little path branching off to the left by the Palm tree on the Main 'Avenue. No servant would ever approach by the Main Drive.

" They worked very hard indeed, especially when the House was full, as it often was. There were rows and rows of water cans to be carried to the bedrooms. Each bedroom had its hip-bath as well as jugs and ewers. Then, every night at least two stone hot bottles had to be taken up to each bedroom.

" And there were the lamps, dozens of them, hand-lamps and wall-lamps and standard ones. Every day they all had to be collected and the glasses cleaned, the wicks trimmed and paraffin put in through a special funnel."

Katie remembers that huge kitchen with its well scrubbed wooden table in the middle, its two large ranges with all the shining copper pots and pans, the tiled floor.

She went on, " Besides all the day-time meals there was always a six-course Dinner in the evening and after it, about Nine o' clock or so, we Staff had our meal in the servants' Hall, not quite the same food as the Dining Room but very good. After

101

it then the baths had to be seen to and all. I enjoyed working up there but I was young in those days. Actually I just went up sometimes to help.

" I remember the Coronation — Edward VII's that is. They gave me a big sack with a stone of raisins in it and told me to stone them. I remember I was just about half-way when they came to say there wasn't to be a coronation as the King had Appendicitis. I don't remember if I ever finished that big bag of raisins!"

My nonagerian friend gazed silently into her cheery coal fire, seeing once more that white kitchen table and the copper pans on the flaming range, her bag of raisins beside her. And, if you're thinking, as I did at first, that all this is very ordinary Edwardian behaviour, remember that this was not a London house nor yet a Stately Home but a relatively humble mansion of the Island of Gigha!

If the Laird and his guests tired of the pleasures of the Library, the Billiard Room and the Drawing Room they could stroll outside to enjoy some of the pleasures of " The Policies — sixty three acres of them which are laid out with much taste and include, besides woodlands and gardens, a Tennis Court, Stables and a Pond as well as the machinery for pumping water to the House." The Tennis Court is now a paddock but otherwise these Policies occupied more or less the same ground as the famous Achamore Gardens do today.

In 1911 the Brochure plan shows " numerous walks through the young plantations which are fast growing into a valuable addition to the amenity of the Residence as well as of the Island." I have talked this matter over with several of the men who worked in these Policies long ago and still work in The Gardens today and they tell me that the general plan is much the same as it was then. Old bushes and trees have been gradually removed to plant more modern Azaleas and Rhododendrons but many of the old bushes and rhododendrons are still in place. Achamore Gardens were definitely not " started from scratch," as I have heard it said, after the Second War but built on the foundation laid out fifty or more years before by W. J. Yorke

Scarlett and his workmen. In fact some of the large beautiful trees at the North-East corner of the Garden were, I am assured, there even before Mr. Scarlett's time.

The Flower Garden, planted with colourful herbaceous plants and Annuals, were labour-intensive. Eonagh (Hugh) Henderson, who still works in the Gardens told me that, as a lad, his job, with another boy, was to keep all the avenues tidy and free from weeds, with rows of primroses planted along the edges. The South Avenue Summer gates of varnished wood had to be changed at the appropriate time for the green Winter Gates. The foot-high box-hedges were neatly trimmed and of course not a weed showed anywhere in any of the extensive beds. And note that all the grass lawns, including the Tennis Court were cut with hand mowers.

Outside the Policies proper, over a hundred acres of land were planted: "*Woods and Woodlands.* These form a most important part of the Estate. They add immensely to the amenity and sport — yielding capabilities of the Island besides affording considerable supplies of wood for fencing and other Estate purposes. The Larch throughout the Plantations shows special promise of growing into useful timber."

So perhaps in time, it was hoped the good people of Gigha would not need to go adventuring on Leim Shore at the time of Divine Service seeking essential building material!

Fishing, both sea and loch, Sea Bathing and Yachting facilities were of course at hand " the sand being white and firm underfoot the facilities for sea bathing cannot be surpassed." What the Brochure does not state is that each year a large tent-like structure erection was put up at Gigulum for the use of the Laird and his guests and here they enjoyed *al fresco* meals complete with large wicker hampers of food.

In view of today's increasing use of Ardminish as a Yachting base the Brochure's statement that " Gigha as a Yachting Base for the West of Scotland is not easily surpassed." is interesting.

That leaves us with the most intriguing Gigha sport of all — Golf. Several people remember that " everyone had a wee few clubs and just went out of an evening." Katie Wilkieson whom we met stoning raisins at the Mansion House, calls to mind the day in 1895 or '96 when the Islay-bound steamer had to wait at the Pier while the match between Gigha Golf Club and the Islay Club was concluded! It was of course to the Golf Course that Sandy Orr galloped yelling "There's flames at Achamore."

On the Golf Course, 1908.

In 1911 the Golf Course stretched in a rough oval from Leim Shore right along the West Course to behind the Lodge. The brochure states that it "was two miles round and, with its natural bunkers is a very sporting and interesting Course while from it can be viewed some of the finest scenery in the district." All this I well believe, it must indeed have been a sporting course!

You may not believe it but I myself, many years ago, long after my father was dead, had quite a lot of fun on, of all places, Turnberry Golf Course with his 'wee few clubs' in a brown canvas golf bag. I had everything necessary, a wooden 'Driver', two Irons and a solid headed putter. In the end I sold them as 'antiques'.

To return to more serious but no less intriguing subjects, to a subject we have studied before; Achamore Farm, John McNeill's old Home Farm. W. J. Yorke Scarlett revived John's policy of having a Home Farm where he appointed a Grieve to carry out improvements to land and stock, which besides being of economic value to himself would serve as an example to the other farmers.

Last time we visited the old place in the 1890's Malcolm McSporran had just died and his widow, Janet, neé

Montgomery, was alone on the Farm. In June 1978 I went to see Miss Mary McNeill who is a grand-daughter of Malcolm and Janet to ask her what happened. " Yes! That's right," she said, after settling me with my coffee and pancake, " Granny was alone and she couldn't manage so Mr. Scarlett suggested that she go down to farm the smaller farm at North Drumachro while Angus Wilkieson, who was at Drumachro go up to Achamore which was to be a Home Farm. And that's what happened." Once more Achamore, which had once been the ancient Chanterioch became the Home Farm which it remained till Major Allen bought Gigha in 1920.

Angus Wilkieson became one of the ' great ' characters of Gigha. You can identify him in the photographs by his gorgeous whiskers and beard. Married to, you will remember, Margaret Galbraith he not only founded one of the Island's most influential families (several in fact) — you've already heard one of his grand-sons Angus Allen reciting ' Flames at Achamore ' as well as watching his daughter-in-law stoning, or not stoning, raisins.

Mansion House, Home Farm, The Lodge, 1908.

Under his management the Home Farm flourished. The 1911 brochure states that the " steading is practically new and is one of the most substantial in Kintyre." Where the old cottages had stood the Gigha workmen built a solid stone open-ended Square of farm buildings whose main function was to house the numerous Clydesdale horses, the key-stone of arable farming. As a reminder of this era the enormous cast-iron trough still stands in the middle of the yard. So important was the breeding of good horses that a Horse Manager was appointed, no less a person that Angus's son, Archie who found a staunch ally in the Factor whose interest in Clydesdales we have already noted.

To get some first-hand information about all this I went along to visit my father's old friend Angus Allen, grand-son of Angus Wilkieson, who has lived all his eighty-three years on Gigha. Comfortably seated beside him I placed the book of photographs on his grey tweed-covered knee. Chuckling appreciatively he turned the pages until he came to the sheep-shearing. " Well I'm dashed " he exclaimed " I never thought to see that picture! What a time we had that day! They weren't sheep shearing at all you know. It was all posed. It took a lot of time arranging everything; the sheep at different stages of shearing and everybody in the right place and then we had to wait till *The Steamer* came in the background. Aye! There were people there as never sheared a sheep in their lives."

Sheep-Shearing, 1908.

" But, Angus," I said " However do you know? Were you there?"

He looked at me, across the book, across the years, his blue eyes twinkling with merriment. Then came the information I had so long wanted but never thought to find.

" See that wee boy keeking through the Fank? That's me. They told me to go away but I was na' going. I didn't see why I shouldn't be in their picture so I just stayed."

He went on to tell me how at first he had spent six years ' in the byres ' at 6/- a week but, tired of being inside all the time, he went down to the Office by the Lodge and asked for a change when he was appointed to serve under his mother Phemie's brother, Archie, among the horses – a post carrying 9/- a week.

" Outside all the time that was much better – with those lovely great Clydesdales. You know I was looking in the paper the other day and I was just thinking of your father because there were two great horses there all done up to go to Canada and they were £20,000. Now I remember up at Achamore your father sold a mare foal of Dunure Footprint. He was one of the big Kintyre stallions. It was said Mr. Philip got £100 for it an unheard of price for a foal.

"We used to take the horses down to Campbeltown Show, me and my Uncle Archie. We had to take them, three or four maybe up to Tarbert and then walk them all the way down to Campbeltown. It was a great job getting these big beasts on and off the Steamer and all the way down the road. We couldn't ride them of course as they had never been off the Island and, if a trap or mebbe a motor had gone buzzing past they'd just have gone birling roun' and roun' all over the road."

He went on to tell me how a good stallion was brought on to the Island each year to serve the mares. Each farm had at least four horses, several had many more.

Every year, to encourage good stock raising, an Agricultural Show was held in the paddock in front of the Home Farm, a wide flat field still known as ' The Show Field.' This was

one of the highlights of Gigha's year with the Kilberry pipers from the Mainland brought by Mr. Scarlett's yacht *The Snapshot.*

Snapshot and all other available boats also brought numerous visitors from Kintyre and from even further afield, while the *Pioneer* made an extra run. The central feature was, of course the parade and judging up at the Home Farm but it seems to me that this was by no means the only object of the Show which was seized as a grand opportunity for would-be buyers of stock to visit farms to inspect animals. After all taking cows and horses to market without being sure of a suitable price or buyer was a risky business. I am given to understand by Angus, and others that " Aye there was a lot of business done that day outside the Show."

In fact the interest in more advantageous farming was not confined to the Home Farm. Steadings were improved all over the Island, many of them being renovated under the direction of the Estate Carpenter, Alexander MacPherson whom Mr. Scarlett had appointed as Inn Charge-Keeper but who previously, besides having been in the Laird's father's Volunteers had had a Master Carpenter's business of his own in Campbeltown. The other workman engaged in all the building was the Estate Mason, none other than our old friend William McSporran, himself Gigha born and bred and married to Catherine Graham. You can see both of them in the photograph of the estate workers.

Willie McSporran's daughter, Susan Orr, remembers as a child taking her father's ' dinner piece ' down to him when he was helping to convert the old ' Gamekeeper's House and Kennels ' into a group of attractive houses in one of which lived John McLaughlan, the Gamekeeper. His duties were concerned with the numerous game birds on the Island and not with a pack of hare-hunting hounds. Susan also remembers that her father was ' working a long time down at Ardlammy.'

Once more an eye-witness account came from Angus Allen who once visited Leim at the turn of the century when he was horrified to find that " it had only a sand floor and no proper walls and just the rafters." However, he told me, that before Robert Andrew, the new tenant, came in 1908 all this had been altered. " And they weren't done when he arrived with his sister and even when he brought his bride they had to live in the Dairy at first. But when they'd finished it was a good house down there at Leim." Mrs. Bicket, the wife of the present tenant of Leim confirmed this opinion when she told me last summer (1978) that Leim farmhouse is an exceptionally well-built house.

On the map accompanying the Brochure the Cottages seem to be very much where they stand today at New Quay, Keill, Gigulum, and Ardminish. In 1911 " they have been entirely re-fitted and several new ones built with stone and lime — with slated roofs — there are now no thatched roofs on the Island."

Direct evidence of the building of one of the Ardminish cottages comes from Miss Mary McNeill who, you recall, told us of Angus Wilkieson's appointment to the Home Farm. She remembers very well that the first year her parents spent in their ' new ' house was 1898 when her brother Duncan was born. I must say we'll meet Duncan when we talk about fishing. The ' new ' house in which he was born is the second one going southwards of the houses in the ' High Street ' — which is exactly what it says, the higher or more westward part of the Village. Miss McNeill told me " It was just one room and kitchen with a loft but, as nobody was allowed summer visitors we had no stairs, just a ladder."

Needless to say Messrs. MacPherson and McSporran did not do all the building. Angus told me how five dyke builders from Campbeltown spent several months on the Island. " Fair daft on building dykes your father was. Like the horses and planting trees he aye went ' at a thing.' They made the dyke from the pier to the Drive and a lot over the fields. Everybody started building dykes round gardens and all!" said Angus with a chuckle, his face creased with merriment.

Before we leave this subject of the buildings, an important one I feel, because the condition of people's houses very often decides the way they can live just look for a moment at an entirely different building. Not a house nor a farm but a new School was erected in 1897. John McNeill's one had stood the Island in good stead for over a hundred years but, by the end of the 19th Century schooling was free and compulsory and the old one was proving less adequate for the increasing demands of

THE HAY CART. *Reproduced by kind permission of the artist, Edna Whyte from Old Rectory Designs, Island of Luing, Argyll.*

new ideas in education. One person on the Island, our old friend Katie Wilkieson is, I think, the one person still living on Gigha today who went to school in that one long room above the Schoolmaster's House with its fireplace at one end.

A deed in the Edinburgh Office dated 1897 signed by W. J. Yorke Scarlett states:— " Considering the School Board of the Parish of Gigha and Cara have executed a disposition in my favour of the Old School House, Teacher's House and Offices held in connection therewith — an area of 2722 square yards. In exchange for the said Disposition I — in terms of the Education (Scotland) Act 1872 — dispose an area of 396 square yards on the South side of the road leading to the present Post Office and the Ferry — on the East side of the Road. The School Board must cause to be built adequate walls and fences round this land — entry will be at Whitsunday 1897." To make up the difference in the amount of land a sum of £300 was ' instantly paid.'

Six years later we find that " that piece of land on which the School now stands does not afford sufficient playground for the scholars I am desirous of granting additional ground therefore I, without any price being paid, — grant 667 square yards — beyond the boundaries of the present playground. — W. J. Yorke Scarlett."

When the new school was completed in about 1898 the Schoolmaster, who you will remember lived below the big schoolroom, swopped with Mr. Cavana who kept the Post Office and Shop down Ferry Road. Mr. Cameron, the Master, went to live in what is now the Ferryman's house while the Cavanas moved to the present Post Office. There they were well-established by 1900 where they conducted their business on the ground floor and converted the Schoolroom into a flat with sitting room, bedrooms, kitchen and bathroom. There they remained till 1912 when Archie Wilkieson, whom we last met when he was Horse Manager at the Home Farm, married Alexander MacPherson's daughter Katie, and they took over the Post Office and made their home upstairs. Soon they added on to the South Gable a store-room with a sitting room above which is now the pleasant

110

room of Seumas and Margaret McSporran the present tenants of the premises – of whom more anon.

Old School, now Shop and Post Office, 1920.

Before we leave the subject of the School and the children I must tell you one tale I heard from both Mary McNeill and Susie Orr, about their childhood. Children in those days, on a farming Island, were very much an integral part of the community. Each had his or her own "job" at home, a job which was vital to that home. They skipped and paddled, messed about in boats, and threw their balls, just as children have done since time immemorial but these pastimes were after their "jobs" were done.

In addition sometimes they could get paid work to augment the family income. One such was "stoning the Clover" which meant you borrowed a large sack apron from your mother and went into the harvest fields to 'howk' the stones from the crops, to help the reapers so that the blades would not get notched. Susie said she had a special small knife for the job but others simply used a sharp stone. The stones they howked out were piled in heaps by the side of the fields. For this you were paid 6d. a day. This you could take home and perhaps be allowed a few pennies to buy sweeties at Sandy Orr's shop in Ardminish Village or up at the Post Office.

At last we have direct evidence of how they lived on Gigha, so far we have been inferring what life was like on the Island. From everyone I asked I heard fascinating details of life at the beginning of this century but the underlying theme was always "Nobody had any money but, money didn't matter in these days." You will remember Mr. Fraser's remark that " nobody bought anything **that** they could go and get." [3]

Listen to Angus Allen first. " Aye things have changed! In the days when I was with my Uncle Archie on the Horses and your Father and Mother were in *The Lodge* we might have been called poor by today's ideas but we weren't. Everybody had enough and plenty of good food. Tatties and Herring and sometimes Cod and Tatties. I remember the wives used to peel and cook a huge pot of potatoes and just tumble the steaming floury heap out into a great dish on the kitchen table and everybody just helped themselves. Every house had a pig in the yard and a few hams hanging from the ceiling and the wife just took a slice when she needed to. Everybody had a few hens scratching away at the doors and of course Milk was cheap or mebbe your neighbour had a cow and you had more hens or something like that. We used to make our own butter and, when the Spring milk came in we had too much cheese and then the Shop couldn't buy it all and that's when we sold it off the Island.

" We used to pile the cheeses, about the size of the one you get up in the Shop today — four or five pounds mebbe and we put them in straw on hurdles and took them down to the Pier where everybody brought theirs to the pile and they took them away on the steamer. That was one way we got money which we had to have to buy things like boots and clothes. A pair of good working boots could cost £2 but they did you for years. When they needed mending Sandy Orr would do them for you. You had to go to Campbeltown for them and for a suit which might cost three or four pounds.

" And of course everybody always had a salted cod or two hanging in the shed on the line. You could fish mackerel or cuddies yourself, everybody had at least a wee boat and there were plenty of rabbits which the farmers were glad for you to take."

112

As I walked back from Angus' home at South Drumachro to the Village, under the lush trees my father had planted, I gazed my fill out towards the gentle hills of Kintyre and the turquoise waters of Gigha Sound. A small fishing boat chugged in towards the Shore. Was it John MacMillan or Duncan McNeill of Tigh Rudh? Whichever of them was in the boat he'd been fishing the seas round Gigha when Cavana was in the Post Office, Archie Wilkieson and Angus Allen were on the horses. It was time I found out about the Fishing community. How did they live? Was what I had heard so far typical only of the farmers?

To find out the answer I climbed up to the High Street to visit Miss Mary McNeill once more, in her house built in 1898. "You want to know what sort of food we had and did we have plenty of money?" she asked. "I don't remember money mattering all that much in the old days. We didn't have many clothes anyway. Everything we had was always good and was well made over but we were always well dressed.

"Oh we all had plenty of food! My father was a fisherman, you know so of course we had fish. Fish for ourselves and for our neighbours. Then we always had a pig or two. My father used to bring one home every spring from a man he knew in Campbeltown and we fed it scraps and things all summer and then, come Autumn, it was killed and smoked and salted so we had meat for the winter. And we'd always plenty of eggs. I remember my mother often used to kill a hen on the Friday or Saturday for my father coming home from the Fishing at the weekend."

She went on to tell me almost exactly the same as Angus Allen. If you had to buy something, say Milk, it was 2d. and at times 1d. a pint. Eggs would be around 2d. a dozen. Rabbits were plentiful for anybody who liked to set a few snares.

My next call was at one of the Cottages in New Quay to see Mrs. Sarah McSporran, who has lived almost all of her eighty years at New Quay.[4] Her parents, Florence and Alexander Graham are, so far as we know, the only couple to have had their wedding on Cara where Florence's father was the Shepherd.

Sarah told me that almost the whole population of Gigha went over that October day in 1893 and "all of them were late for work the next morning." Ten years later after five children, including Sarah had been born, her father Alexander Graham, a fisherman, was drowned in a sudden storm off Cara. A few months afterwards another son was born.

"This," said Sarah, "left my mother without a man to bring in wood and do the house. Not having much money wasn't so bad but you needed a man to go down to the Shore to get wood from wrecks and to fetch the big bits from the coal boats who sometimes brought it in. Then they could make proper floor and ceilings and walls. We were one of the last houses to have a sand floor and very rough wood in the roof, until my brothers got older. It was really only one room then with a partition for the kitchen." She looked proudly round her well-decorated room with its small kitchen next door and a bedroom downstairs with proper attic rooms. The coal fire burned merrily in the modern grate.

"We cooked on that fire, open it was then, with a swee at one side with a long arm you swung over the fire and hooks to hang the pots and the kettle on. You had different sizes of hooks depending on how quick you wanted it to boil.

"Water? Oh we got all that from the well out there. We did all our washing out there in big wooden tubs. We trod the blankets." She laughed gaily and raised her skirt to demonstrate with a little dance step. She dropped her skirt and rose. "Have another cup of coffee? There you are now! She sat down again. "It was hard work but we enjoyed it. When we washed them we wrung them with an old broom handle. You took the broom head off and one of you held the blanket at the edge of the tub and the other twisted the blanket round and round. Then we hung it over the dyke by the Leim road — the dykes were clean in those days — or on the bushes and spread it to dry in the wind and the sun. If the water was short we went down to the wee burn that runs between Leim and Drumachro and made a dam with stones. We took the big iron pot with the three legs and washed down there. We had time — time to work and to play and time to go to see a sick friend or a lonely person."

She sighed and poked up the already blazing fire. "Clothes you want to know about? Oh! We got what we wanted from a man who came round. He had a book with patterns of dresses and things, stockings and underclothes and you told him what you wanted and he brought what you ordered the next time he came and you paid him. He had patterns of material too and, if you wanted a dress he measured you and you chose your pattern and your stuff and, the next time he came he brought your dress."

One thing the people of Gigha, be they fishermen or farmers, cottagers, or crofters will always join in with alacrity is any kind of rejoicing. In the close-knit community one person's joy or, for that matter sorrow, was everybody's.

Not only was I told the recurrent theme about money not really mattering but over and over again "the pairties we used to have," kept recurring. At most of those the chief delicacy appears to have been, to my surprise, "Tatties and Herring and Oatcakes," "The Oatcake," I was told, "was just to put your herring on." and again "The right way to eat a herring was to put it on an oatcake and pick the flesh off with your fingers." and "I've seen my father and his brothers pick a herring cleaner of flesh than wi' a knife. Jist the bones left they were." Two annual dances took place, one was the Harvest Home Dance up at Achamore while the other was the Christmas Party in the School, where the Laird's presents were distributed. The Harvest Home Dance was up in the big barn above the Steading — above the Bothy which is now a store-room. The music would be provided by Fiddlers with an occasional accordian, while Donald the Blind Piper, grand-son of Alexander McNeill the Ferryman would play if he were at home. Dashing White Sergeants, Eightsome Reels, Gay Gordons exhausted the company who might then be entertained by a star performer doing a Sword Dance or the Highland Fling. Food was generously provided, roast beef, tatties, 'clouty Dumplings' — and of course plenty of drink of varying degrees of hardness. [5]

Other days too were attended by celebrations. Days like the Show Day and of course the Annual Ploughing Match where as many as twelve ploughs with 24 horses competed for the coveted medals. The record was held, Angus Allen tells me, by Angus Wilkieson of the Home Farm who won the " Gold Medal" in 1894, '97, '98, and '99. That evening, besides parties all over the Island a Grand Dinner was held in the Hotel for the Judges from the Mainland and the officials and prizewinners. [6]

In view of the interest on Gigha today in Sales of Work and suchlike let me just tell you about a fascinating account of a Sale in 1916 or '17 which I found in a fisherman's Account Book kept by Malcolm McNeill, Betty's father. Among catches of Lobsters and Cod I read: " A well organised and highly successful Free Gift Sale held for the Red Cross took place at Tarbert Farm on the 8th Ult. The gifts were disposed of by Mr. Wilson the Auctioneer from Paisley. Everybody contributed while some sent donations and many gifts." The list of gifts is worth noting! Donations of livestock included several calves " quey calves and one bull calf." Fowls, Ducks and drakes were for sale " at good prices," as well as numerous dozens of eggs, cheeses, bags of potatoes and " a hundredweight of fish." Naturally people sent a variety of jars of jelly which were sold as well as several pairs of gloves and knitted socks, six walking sticks and five pipes. Even more astonishing " a number of articles bought were re-sold after the Sale, raising thereby more money."

Further to our adventures on the Sacramental Week-end let me add, finally, this account from Katie Wilkieson of such a week-end a hundred years later.

" We had a whole lot of Ministers on Gigha for Communion. Maybe five or six from the Mainland, from different parishes. We had a lot of Services but the chief ones were divided into those for Gaelic speakers and those for English speakers. On the Thursday, that is the Preparation Day, the English speakers got their Tokens. We still use them. We don't have cards but these old round tokens. I think they're very old. They got them at the Preparation Service. The Gaelic people got theirs at the Morning Service on the Saturday.

" On the Communion Sunday the Gaelic people had their Service in the Church at 12 o' clock. The Communion Table ran down the whole length of the Church, and was covered with a white cloth. Some of the pews were covered with white cloths too. When it came the time for the Communion those in the pews that weren't covered came to the table and also the folk sitting up in the galleries, one at each end. We had two Cups, very old Pewter cups. Nowadays we have two silver ones. But then they were Pewter.

" The English-speaking people had their Service up in the School and, after the Gaelic people had finished they came out and the English people went in for their Communion. Then the English people came out and the Gaelic people went in for their Thanksgiving Service. Everybody came back for a united Thanksgiving Service in the evening, about six o' clock.

" The collection at the Gaelic Service was taken up in great big wooden ladles with long handles but the collection at the English Service was put in salvers laid on the table. I used to go to the Gaelic Services after I joined the Church. Of course we didn't join till we were grown up. Most girls joined when they were married. A bride always had one really good black silk dress and she wore this always to the Communion. I remember watching them from the windows in the Hotel. When I went I had a French Prayer Book and I heard the Service in the Gaelic, thought of it in English and followed it in French. We had a French mistress in the School. She gave me the book."

Well, we've romped through the 19th Century, onward ever onward. We've seen that the wave of success that appeared to be gathering at the end of the 18th had flattened out in the mid-19th. Luckily hidden strength lay, as it always does, hidden even in the trough and, in due course, the first fourteen years of the 20th Century throbbed with life on Gigha.

The Summer of 1914 was splendid. In the Spring the Clydesdales ploughed the fields, the seed sown was growing well, Midsummer was as jocund as ever. The births of two babies were celebrated, a daughter for Mr. and Mrs. Andrew down in the well-built house at Leim,[7] a first child for the Factor and his wife at the Lodge.[8] Horses went to Campbeltown Show. The Kilberry pipers played stirring music up at the Show Field at the Home Farm as the Parade slowly wound past the Laird's Party on the dais. At the Mansion House preparations went forward for the beginning of Pheasant Shooting in August.

Then the wave broke, that tidal wave which had been gathering momentum in Europe for many years. Slowly, but surely, the people of Gigha were engulfed in its terrible force.

I've asked several friends about the War but all I was told was " the men went away and some of them didn't come back." or " We all knitted like mad." or " No! We were never very short of anything in the food line." As nobody seemed to have any stories to tell me I'll tell you a couple of my own to cheer up the end of this chapter which has been lit by living memory.

Once more, at the height of the submarine menace, ships of War lurked in the Sound of Gigha, that insignificant strategically-placed little Island. One very dark night my mother, wishing to pick some flowers for departing guests, seized my father's big lantern and went out into the garden in front of the Lodge. The guests were just leaving with their large bunch of flowers when the sound of running feet came up the avenue. A party of naval men rushed in. Someone had been Signalling from here to a Submarine which must be in the Bay. A Spy was loose somewhere. Who was it? I gather it took all my mother's Irish blarney and a certain amount of my father's Whisky to talk them out of that one!

Finally allow me one memory of my own, my very first clear memory. I stood in front of one of our dining room chairs the Daily paper spread on the seat. With a spit-wetted chubby finger I rubbed the thick black lines down the pages — lots of thick black lines which could be transferred to my face, making lovely patterns. When mother appeared I gathered this was " Naughty." — which didn't surprise me. What *was* odd and has always stuck in my memory was that it was " Naughty to the poor dead soldiers." It was many years before I discovered that my black lines were printed down the long columns of the names of those killed on the battlefield.

By the time the dead had all been counted and the War was officially over, as one Gigha friend remarked " These days had all gone bye." I don't exactly know what happened but the Scarlett money was not so plentiful after the War so in 1919 the Island was sold to Major John Allen. Major Allen had been a frequent visitor in ' the old days.' He and his family were very fond of the Island but, in the aftermath of War, misfortune dogged them after they came to Gigha. Once more it began to appear as though Winter was setting in again on Gigha.

But you and I have seen, over and over again that on Gigha Winter is short and mild and Spring comes with promise of a bountiful Summer. Whether Gigha means ' God's Island ' or not I just don't know but I do know it could with justice mean the fortunate Island.

BACK ROW (Left to Right): H. Smith, A. Milloy, J. Campbell, Archie Wilkieson, Alexander Graham.

NEXT ROW (Standing): Angus Wilkieson, N. Graham, A. Graham, D. Clark, Donald MacDonald, Neil Galbraith, A. McGeachy, J. McLauchlan, W. W. Philip.

3rd ROW (Seated): A. MacMillan, Alex McPherson, Wm. McSporran, J. Cavana, Capt. McCallum.

SEATED ON GROUND: Angus Wilkieson, M. Graham.

Chapter 9—Gigha today
The Flourishing Island

What of Gigha today? What has been happening on the Island since W. J. Yorke Scarlett sold it in 1920 to Major John Allen? To be quite sure our knowledge is accurate and up to date I decided to return once more to the Island to let it speak for itself. Now, in September 1978, I am writing this at the window above the Shop. Out there, in Ardminish Bay three elegant white yachts ride at anchor where Haco's ill-fated fleet rested in the Thirteenth Century. Once, or perhaps more than once, that aquamarine water was churned by raiders like Alan na Sop while the white sand was stained red with blood as beasts were dragged off and Gigha men slain.

Thinking of more peaceful matters I looked round Margaret McSporran's pleasant Dining Room and thought of the days a couple of hundred years ago when John Galbraith, Schoolmaster and Session Clerk sharpened his quills and mixed his ink powder in this very room before he sat down to write the Session Records, little thinking of their value for the history of Gigha. Here, too, several generations of Gigha children learned their Reading and Spelling and did their sums when this whole flat was their Schoolroom. In fact where I was sitting in the window used to be the rows of desks where the ' big ' girls sat with the boys along the opposite wall and the master sat in his high chair at the end where the fireplace was.

I began by making a list of the topics which have particularly interested us and then set out to visit my various friends on the Island to discover the latest news about them.

By this time I hope you will agree that the Proprietor is one of the most important factors in the progress or otherwise of the Island so, as I wended my way through the village on my way up to Achamore I thought of the men who had succeeded Mr. Scarlett. In due course Major Allen, who had bought Gigha from him, passed it on to his son John who died shortly afterwards and it was sold, in 1937, to R. J. A. Hamer Esq. who, in turn sold it three years later to Somerset de Chair Esq., whose wife was a Miss Hamer, who held it during the disastrous years of the Second War. For a short time it indeed looked as though Gigha, like Britain itself, had come to the end of its prosperity.

Then, quite suddenly, the old pattern repeated itself, just as it had done in the time of John McNeill and W. J. Yorke Scarlett: Gigha was sold to Sir James Horlick, a man, not only with a keen business sense but with a deep appreciation of beautiful places and things. He it was who built on John McNeill's foundations and Yorke Scarlett's improvements to achieve Gigha's flourishing state today. He lived on Gigha till his death, in Achamore House, in 1972. Finally, in 1974 Gigha became the property of D. W. Landale Esq., who is the present Proprietor.

To understand the position of Gigha today you and I will be well-advised to glance for a moment at the significant policy and actions of Sir James. Having modernised his Mansion House he filled it with priceless furniture and antiques. Spaces were created in the Scarlett garden for gorgeous Azaleas and exotic Rhododendrons as well as many more unusual shrubs. In addition, and perhaps his most important action so far as the people of Gigha were concerned, Sir James set up the Gigha Creamery Company on which depends the economic prosperity of the Island today.

Probably it would be true to say that Sir James's collection of priceless antiques did not affect the life of the tenants very much but we have already followed the varied fortunes of Achamore House through the years so that I thought you might like the story brought up-to-date. His collection of 18th Century painted glass plates, framed in Chinese Chippendale, themselves extremely precious and rare, was world famous. His priceless Jade pieces were, I am told by his grandson David Wagg "bought because he liked them and not because they made a collection in themselves." Antique needlework fascinated him

122

and still in the House stands a great bed whose ornate headpiece and cover were embroidered to the order of Louis XIV of France for his mistress Madame de Maintenon. This is such a rarity that, recently a party of needlewomen came to see it all the way from America. Strangely enough Sir James actually bought it in America where it had been brought from the Corsini Palace in Florence. On the lovely oak floors he laid fabulous rugs and carpets, mostly from Samarkand while on his specially erected bookcases stood Sir James's amazing collection of rare books, mostly prints of birds and flowers, plates of rare and colourful beauty.

Incidentally David Wagg tells me he and his family are at a loss to understand why the Kintyre Commissioners include plates of the old fireplaces in their report as these were bought from a dealer in London and have no connection with either Gigha or Scotland. I add this before someone thinks they come from an old house on Gigha itself! On Sir James's death his priceless treasures were dispersed and another chapter in the history of Achamore had closed.

The saga by no means ended there. For a time after Mr. Landale bought the Island the House was in use as part of the Hotel which was being entirely modernised and extended. Knowing all this I gladly accepted an invitation to tea with the Wardens of the House today, Mr. and Mrs. McKenzie. The deep patina of the oak pannelling, the floor boards and the wonderful staircase shines with polishing. Colourful and dignified modern curtains drape the high windows. Only one fireplace remains in the Drawing Room which, to my mind has been enhanced by the removal of the Edwardian tables and knick-knacks. Its spaciousness is emphasised by comfortable modern sofas on the antique Axminster carpet with its soft blues and pinks.

The real change in the House lies in the kitchen where the old work room has been entirely modernised and as I watched some workmen installing a large dish-washing machine I couldn't help remembering Katie Wilkieson's account of the scullery maids washing all the dishes and pots after the late six-course Dinner. This new kitchen is an important part of the present arrangements for the use of the Laird's Mansion. A flat has been reserved for the use of himself and his family during their frequent visits to the Island. Another is available for letting while the rest of the large House is being used as a Conference Centre of which Mr. and Mrs. MacKenzie are Wardens. Mr. MacKenzie also acts as Mr. Landale's representative in his absence.

Refreshed by my welcome and much cheered by what I had seen in Achamore House I walked back down through the Gardens which we last saw being planted with 'useful timber,' Rhododendrons, Delphiniums, Antirrhinums and other colourful herbaceous flowers, Palm trees and Pampas. Now, as a result of Sir James's additions and modifications the Achamore Gardens on Gigha, where all the plants belong to the National Trust, are one of the glories of the Western Isles.

Strangely enough this famous part of the policies is by no means the only flourishing section of the Gardens. Away up in the Kitchen Garden half-a-dozen Gigha men grow literally hundredweights of fruit and vegetables for the House and the Hotel. In fact one of the Gardeners told me that one of the most popular subjects for photographs last Summer was the Red Currant bushes which were clothed in bright shining lace curtains of juicy red fruit which visitors, strictly forbidden in the Garden, could just see round the top of a path.

Fortunately for the general welfare of the people of Gigha, Sir James was a very prescient business man as well as a wealthy one. Let me tell you about the Gigha Creamery Company. The Creamery was started up at Achamore for Cheese making in 1942 by the Ministry of Food, being run in fact by the Scottish Milk Marketing Board. In 1952 it was taken over by Mr. Farquharson of Islay who also held the Islay Creamery. Six years later, thanks to the efforts of Sir James Horlick, the Gigha Creamery Company was formed whereby the farmers of the Island held 49% of the shares while the Proprietor held 51%. Mr. Landale still adheres to this arrangement.

In 1955 the milk production was over 141,000 gallons and twenty-two years later it had risen to 386,000 gallons. In that year 195 tons of Gigha Cheese were produced and sent to the Company of Scottish Cheesemakers in Glasgow as well as being sold locally. All this has been written down for me by

Robert Blackwood of Ardlammy who is a Director of the Company. Mr. Blackwood also adds that they are hoping to start a whey-butter making process in 1979.

Mr. Blackwood was on holiday when I was on the Island but I was fortunate in having long conversations with Neil Bannatyne, himself a native of Gigha, who is responsible for the milk collection itself. He not only drives the Tanker to collect the milk but keeps all the day-to-day records. I met him and his Tanker one day when I was motoring up to the North End. Gigha road being made for one way traffic, we both drew on to the grass above Tarbert Bay. Trying to keep my eyes from wandering off to that superlative view of the blue sea, the dark Paps of Jura with the slopes of Kintyre on the other side, Neil told me that one of his main problems at the moment is that all the machinery, including his own Arithmetic is geared to gallons, not litres, which causes much calculation especially as one gallon of milk, if properly processed, makes one pound of cheese. The tentacles of the Common Market have reached even to Gigha!

Neil's uncle John, brother of the last Blacksmith of Gigha, first drove the milk to the Creamery in churns in a four-wheeled wagon in the 1940's. His record delivery was on June 3rd 1948 when he took 503 gallons to Achamore. Today Neil delivers some 1100 to 1700 gallons each day. I became somewhat bemused by all these statistics but one remark Neil made did stick in my head. He has a letter from the Milk Marketing Board to notify him that the milk production increase of Gigha farmers last year — 13% — was by far the highest in the British Isles.

It was at my next meeting with Neil and his Tanker that I experienced one of those never-to-be forgotten moments that illuminate the life of every local historian. One brilliantly sunny morning I walked along to South Drumachro to call on our old friend Angus Allen. You will remember Angus who started work at Achamore at 'the byres' at 6/- a week before he was promoted to the horses. I had just sat down beside him when a rumbling in the Yard told us that Neil and his Tanker had arrived. Angus collected his cap and we went out into the yard where Neil was just connecting the tanker hose to the refrigerator milk container in Angus's Dairy. As we all stood and watched the two hundred and sixty gallons of creamy milk being sucked into the tanker suddenly Angus chuckled, his blue eyes twinkling brightly, " I remember the day," he said, " I first took my milk up to the Creamery in the cart. I had two churns with eight gallons in each. At the end of the month we had a cheque for £60 but I took it back to them as I didn't think you could get all that money for milk but it was mine all right. And that month I'd sold a cow for £14. My! I was over the moon! I thought I was a rich man that day! Aye! Times have changed!"

Irresistably drawn to go to see the hub of Gigha's economic prosperity I plodded up once more to Achamore Farm where part of the Steading has been extended and adapted for the Creamery. Fascinated, I watched Mr. Little, the Manager, and one of his assistants drawing a huge frame, rather like an outsize comb through an enormous vat of creamy curds. He told me that, very early in the morning, they pour the previous day's milk into these vats, add a carefully measured quantity of Rennet and then do this criss-cross cutting to make it easier to separate the curds from the whey. Gradually the temperature is raised while a swinging bar churns the curds round and round for some two hours when the whey is dried out. Before being put into the actual cheese-mill the curds are again cut up, salted and cooled when they are placed in muslin lined moulds and systematically pressed before being left to mature. Mr. Little tells me that sometimes they add a small quantity of orange colouring because, for some reason, the customer prefers coloured cheese although it makes no difference to the flavour. Besides the large cheeses they make a quantity of smaller cheeses for sale in the local shop. Beginning as it did with the good Gigha grass, the expert build-up of herds, the scrupulously clean milking, this whole process, from start to finish struck me as an extremely scientific and expert business. Between grass and the delicious cheese so many technical factors are involved, so many possible variations of temperature and timing that I came away from Achamore with a new respect for the skill of Gigha farmers and the expertise of Mr. Little and his assistants.

As I meandered along the Road back towards the Village I thought of the farms. Together we have seen clachans become farm complexes still bearing the old names, fifteen in the early Nineteen hundreds. Today North and South Drumachro are worked together as are North and South Ardminish, Tarbert and Highfield, Ardailly and Drumeonmore. The others are more or less as we last saw them although more and more land is being brought under cultivation with the aid of modern earth and stone moving machinery. Four of the farms have modern Milking Parlours while at least two more may have them by the time you read this book. Each farm, although sending its milk to the Creamery is a separate economic unit with herds of upwards of sixty cows as well as beef cattle and sheep.

One thing I envy the people of Gigha is their milk. Each day, around tea-time I see them carrying home plastic milk cans full of fresh milk, still warm from the cows. One modern abomination does not exist on the Island — Pasteurised milk and almost the only commodity not sold in Gigha Shop is everlasting milk in nasty cardboard containers!

I sauntered past the path leading to Woodside, the former home of the Gamekeeper where several families live in modern cottages. Past the three newish bungalows on the right I stopped to chat to Archie Bannatyne, the old Smith, as he emerged from his smart Doran House built exactly on the site of the old Smiddy. The entire rebuilding of Ardminish Village was another of the successful projects carried out by Sir James Horlick. As well as the houses down on the road some new ones were erected up on the High Street in one of which lives Nurse Allee with, in her garden a small surgery for Doctor Thoms from the Mainland when he visits the Island once a week, as well as by specialists like a Chiropodist and an Oculist. Being the Nurse on Gigha carries very special responsibilities. Unlike nurses on the Mainland Nurse Allee, and her assistant, Mrs. Dorothy Wilkieson, cannot summon a doctor in an emergency, especially if anything happens on a dark and stormy night — as such accidents tend to do! Apart from a cool head she must have an expert knowledge of modern drugs and methods.

In fact it was very early one morning last year that one of the farmer's sons sustained a terrible cut with a machine he was working. Nurse was telephoned and Gigha's emergency Service swung into action. Dr. Thoms was alerted, and the Ferryman. The McSporran taxi was immediately made into an ambulance, the official (part-time-voluntary) stretcher party called out. The boy was taken from Tarbert farm to the Ferry, bleeding profusely from an abdominal cut. Nurse staunched the bleeding all the way over on what must have seemed a long half-hour. There at Tayinloan Dr. Thoms awaited them with the appropriate treatment. The Campbeltown Ambulance rushed him to the airport from where he was flown to Glasgow. I saw him only the other day, some six months later cheerfully helping in a field. You may ask why a helicopter was not called. Simply that, by the time the crew have been persuaded, in the absence of a doctor, that it is needed the Emergency Service of Gigha and Campbeltown can have the patient in hospital!

So far so good but remember, if the Ferry cannot cross the Nurse's knowledge may mean the difference between life and death. When I see Nurse Allee driving around the Island in her neat blue Mini with her jaunty hat and trim uniform I cannot help remembering tales of my own mother, who was a Queen's Nurse as they called them in those days, cycling around the Island on a sit-up-and beg bike with a candle in her lamp. Her skirts were long and on her head was tied a black bonnet. If she wanted to summon a doctor she had to light a bonfire up on a hill hoping he could see it and that he would appear in due course. That was in 1910 or so! Not only that but, before she married she lived away down at Leim which is not so convenient as Nurse Allee's house at Ardminish!

Next door to the Nurse's House live Mr. and Mrs. John MacMillan. John is one of the last of the older fishermen left on the Island today so, remembering that it was his good memory which led us to the 1911 Brochure, I called there one evening to ask him about the decline in Gigha's Fishing industry. In Mr. Fraser's time sixty men were engaged in Herring fishing alone, not counting other fishing. In the Nineteenth Century the numbers dwindled from fifty in the 1840's to only just over twenty. Today only two men on Gigha are engaged in full-time fishing. Angus MacAlistair tends his Lobster Creels while Ian Wilkieson catches Clams.

Johnnie, as he is universally called, told me about the thirty feet long Loch Fyne skiffs from which they fished earlier this century. Four men could sleep, below decks, where they cooked on a small coal stove. " Later we got the Paraffin." he remarked. Motive power was provided by sails and " great heavy oars which we had to use cross-handed to make headway. In 1915 we got motors. They were tricky at first. You see they had no reverse but were straight drive so you had to have plenty of room if you wanted to go the other way."

" The names of the boats you want to know? Well there was the *Jessie Jane* with me and my brother James and the *Janet* with Betty's father Malcolm and his brother Duncan McNeill who is still living at Tigh Rudh. Donald, along the row there, he fished from the *Renown*, that was their new boat. The Wotherspoon boat was *Molly Dhom*, Brown Molly and then there was the *Ocean Queen*, she's the one that's lying rotting down at Galloichille. I had a smaller boat, the *Lady Bell*. She slept two.

" We spent the whole year at the Fishing, in a manner of speaking. From February till May we were at the Cod. We fished with a line of 900 hooks baited every day. At first we used Buckie's, later we used bits of the Cod. Then from May till the weather broke we fished the Lobsters. All over Christmas till February again we had our gear to overhaul, our boats and our nets and making creels. For the cod we'd go away to Islay or Jura or Tayvallich for mebbe three or four weeks but for the Lobsters we just fished our own coasts.

" The end of the Cod fishing came one day at the beginning of the War, the Second one that is, when a boat called the *Destine of Dublin* fouled all our nets. They gave us just £7 in compensation. We were finished! Some of us went out again of course. Then towards the end of the War one year four of us spent the Winter as usual doing our boats and gear and then we fished the Cod from February till the end of May and at the end of it all we had exactly 3/6 each man for all our months and months of work. Three of us just went to the Pub. Only one kept his! That was the end of Gigha's Cod fishing."

Johnnie still goes to his creels and I watched him one morning coming in across Ardminish Bay. I went down to meet him. " How many today, Johnnie?" I asked. " Just one," he replied. " They are spoiling the Lobsters too with these big winching cranes with their huge creels out in the deep water which they can winch up. Just scraping the bottom of all the Lobsters so none are coming into our shallower waters. I've brought something here to show you if I met you." He drew a small notebook from his pocket. " I've got the numbers of my catches here. Where's my record? Here it is! In one week in August 1945 two of us got 461 Lobsters just across off Jura."

I am sorry that the actual evidence is so sparse compared with the facts we have concerning farms. Nobody measured the ' acreage ' of a fishing ground or the exact returns for the labour put into the work of this once great occupation of Gigha. Moreover, as far as I can see, no proprietor could do very much to help the fishermen as he could the farmers. The hard fact is that however good the Cod Banks off Gigha or plentiful the Lobsters no harvest from the sea could bring as high a profit as the produce of the good Gigha grass. Certainly in our century it is difficult to see if anything at all could be done to halt the decline in fishing. Boats like the *Destine of Dublin* have now become involved in a Cod War in which few remember the first casualties, the *Janet*, the *Jessie Jane*, the *Molly Dhom*, the *Renown*, and the *Ocean Queen*, the Loch Fyne skiffs of Gigha.

On my way back from the MacMillan home in Ardminish I paused a moment to sit on the dyke opposite the Hotel partly to pay my respects to the site of the Old Church, partly to ruminate on the changes in the Hotel itself. From the front, being a Scheduled building it looks much the same as when John McNeill built it at the end of the Eighteenth Century but inside it was completely altered just after Mr. Landale came. That was when Achamore House was used as an annexe. One day in the Summer Mr. and Mrs. Landale took me over it. The entrance is now at the side where an arched door leads into a spacious reception hall. A Lounge and Cocktail bar are connected by a hatch with the main bar around the walls of which hang framed prints of the photographs of old Gigha, many of them lent by residents, some of which are from Charles Reid's book. An extension has been built comprising a long and cheerfully furnished Dining Room for about forty people above which are comfortable modern bedrooms. The new kitchen, need I say, is completely modernised.

Perhaps the most intriguing of the innovations is the Yachtsmen's part where men from the sea can enjoy a bath a luxurious wash and brush up, not only for themselves but their wet clothes in the special rooms fitted with washing machines and tumble driers. Meanwhile of course the sailors themselves can enjoy a drink in the well-stocked bar and then have a delicious meal in the Dining Room. This comfortable modern hostelry is pleasantly and capably managed by Mr. and Mrs. Ken Roebuck. Incidentally their Staff, like the staff at the Creamery and the Gardens are all Gigha people.

Leaving my seat on the dyke opposite the Hotel I set off once more for the Shop. Just as I reached it I met Miss Rigley, the Headmistress of the School. Eagerly I accepted her invitation to ' look over ' the School so, together we set off down the Ferry Road. The building, cheerfully decorated, contains three classrooms in all, but one of these is now used as a dining room where all thirty-four scholars have dinner each day, cooked by Mrs. Henderson who lives in the Village. Both the classrooms used as such are well equipped with tables and chairs to suit the ages of the children who work there. All around I saw the usual material for modern teaching but, what really caught my attention, was the project in the more senior class room on Iona, complete with a model Cathedral in the making, the rudiments of a beehive hut and a coracle not to speak of a well drawn large map. Just imagine doing a project on Iona in a large classroom whose picture windows look away to the South, over Gigha, over the sea to the Mull of Kintyre!

My attention was caught by another wall display — and remember nobody had known I was coming. I met Miss Rigley by chance! There was a large hand-drawn map of Gigha itself surrounded by ' essays ' written by the children. Actually what attracted my ex-school ma'am's attention was the excellence of the spelling and punctuation, the neatness of the writing.

Whether they go to Oban or Campbeltown Secondary school these children will be a credit to their teachers on Gigha. ı.

I read some of the pieces which were written about what they would like to see done to improve the Island. Almost all thought more jobs should be created although some of the ideas were unusual: " I'd build a roll-on-roll-off Ferry so that the men could build it and the ladies could get work making tea for them." Other suggestions which I feel would have appealed to W. J. Yorke Scarlett's ideas of doing two things at once: local labour could " build houses for the old people " or " Build a landing pad for a helicopter on top of the Surgery." or (a very popular suggestion) " make a Leisure Centre with a football pitch and a Swimming pool." One lass thought all roads should be council roads with paths beside them for cyclists and walkers " but not too much as we don't want it to be like Glasgow."

Nearly half of them wanted a Secondary School on the Island " so we won't have to go away." One boy thought " none of the views should be spoilt " or " I'd improve it but not too much as the people who live here wouldn't like it." The one I thought revealing was over a name of a child whom I know is not a native " Gigha is a nice place and I like to live in it as it is."

Feeling that I agreed heartily with the girl I walked slowly back up towards the Shop to write up my day's adventures but, by the time I had eaten Margaret McSporran's delicious supper I sat idly by the fire in her sitting room, built on to the old School to make a store for the shop on the lower storey and a cosy sitting room above. I just sat and thought about the Shop.

The Gigha Shop at Ardminish run by Margaret and Seumas (James) McSporran is, to my mind, one of the pivotal points of modern Gigha.[4] Seumas, by the way, is a grandson of William McSporran that man whom we first met as a child of four at Achamore in the 1860's and later as the Estate Mason. His mother is another friend, Sarah down at New Quay who trod her blankets and cooked on a swee. Thus he is a living example of our earlier discussion about the mingling of old and new families on Gigha today. On the same theme his wife, Margaret comes from England as indeed at least four of the wives of farmers, themselves Gigha men, were born on the Mainland of Britain.

To return to the Shop. Just on sixteen years ago the husband and wife partnership of Seumas and Margaret acquired the Island's Post Office and Shop which had been run, in the Scarlett days first by John Cavana and then by the Wilkiesons, all the time expanding as more and more commodities were required on the Island until today they stock, in their mini-supermarket, a quite astounding selection of goods from Butter to Wellingtons, from Butcher Meat to Stationery. Nor, so far as I can gather are all the available goods in the Shop window, so to speak. I've met several people for whom Seumas has brought back electrical goods of one kind or another and fixed them in position for the customer. I even met one mother who proudly showed me a bicycle with a special basket seat into which she can safely strap her little disabled son so that she can ride to her part-time work or do her shopping and visit friends. It was she who said " If you want anything just ask Seumas. He'll bring it back for you and see it's working before he leaves!"

Notice that verb " bring." All the goods in the Shop with few exceptions, as well as anything else required by his customers has to be conveyed to the Island by Seumas and his white van. This entails meticulous organisation not only of lists of goods (Seumas tells me he has to make lists of his lists!) but arranging the transport of himself and his van to and from the Island by the *Pioneer*. I hope in time that many copies of this book will travel to Gigha in that van!

Seumas is also official Police Officer, Fire Officer, Coastguard, Harbour Master, Registrar, and Undertaker to name but a few of his posts. For all of these Margaret is his deputy when he is off the Island fetching supplies. In addition the McSporran cars are the school transport, the Ambulance, the hearse as well as the Gigha Taxi fleet! In case they have too much free time this cheerful couple run a small guest house in the comfortable house made from the old School-room. Their two children, Margaret and Alisdair are becoming a real help in this project. Their special job is to service and line up each morning the fleet of bicycles of all colours, ages and sizes so that the visitors can hire them to ride around the Island. The partnership of Seumas and Margaret is indeed one of the outstanding features of life in the flourishing Island today. Long may it continue to be so!

To continue our list of topics I suggest we go and look at Gigha's ' new ' Church. Up on the hill opposite the shop stands the dignified black whinstone building. In the Session Minutes it is recorded that a fund had in fact been set up for such a Church before the First War but, like so many other projects that one had to be postponed.[1] Not till 1923 was this Church built and opened. The Consecration cross and the date are on the North wall of the Chancel.

I chose a rather gloomy day to climb the path and enter by the front door. My attention was rivetted by the glowing jewelled colours of the windows. I doubt if any other small church has such a wealth of modern stained-glass windows. Pausing for a moment by the newest, a memorial to Sir James Horlick, not surprisingly a light window, its centre piece a tree of life, I was drawn to the most spectacular one of all. This is the memorial to Kenneth McLeod who was minister of the Parish from 1923 to 1948. A golden-crowned crimson-robed David plays a Celtic harp while smaller vignettes show St. Brigid and her cow, a green-robed St. Patrick, the brown coracle of St. Columba while a delightful scene of blue sea, green hills and a flying white seagull suggests the Sound of Gigha.

The Inscription records that Kenneth McLeod was a " Pastor, Preacher and Poet." It is indeed an impressive window but I cannot feel it truly portrays that " very parfitt knight " who translated so sensitively the Songs of the Hebrides and composed the most loved Scottish March, *The Road to the Isles*.

My own favourite is the simple window, in soft sea-weedy colours to Donald MacFarlane who was minister from 1907 to 1923. The large, almost life-size figure of St. Columba in a brown robe kneels on the shore, his hands are raised in utter devotion as his eyes gaze into the heavens. Behind him his coracle rides at anchor. Unlike the McLeod window the simplicity of the kneeling figure recalls Donald MacFarlane as I knew him.

I had just reached the two little windows of Mary and Martha in memory of two of my own old friends, Margaret and Jennie McNeill, grand-daughters of the Ferryman when I heard steps behind me. I turned to meet the present minister, the Reverend James Robertson. Together we looked at the ancient Font which has been brought from Kilchattan to be used in the present Church.

" We've got a lovely Scottish silver bowl which fits exactly inside as the stone one had a hole in it. Would you like to see it? Come along and I'll show you some treasures!"

So off the two of us set to the Church Safe which Mr. Robertson unlocked and drew out a green baize bag. " here it is — hand-beaten Scottish Silver." He handed me a truly exquisite modern piece of silver, shaped to fit the font exactly. From another box he drew two handsome silver cups, the Communion Cups used today in the Service but then he reached further back into the safe to draw out the valuables I had longed to see. I lifted, reverently, I'm not ashamed to admit, one of the enormous pewter Communion Cups, each one of which holds well over a pint. I was holding one of the ancient Communion Cups of Gigha and Cara Parish which were in use in the Reverend Fraser's time and for over a century and a half thereafter. These were the very cups which had held that wine which had been brought from Campbeltown at the end of the Eighteenth Century from which the " worthy " members of the Congregation and their friends from the Mainland had drunk inside the Church while the preaching went on in the Tent!

Mr. Robertson placed a tall black tin box on the table. " Now! See what's in that!" I put the cup down and took the lid off the box and tipped its contents into my hand. Out tumbled with a dull rattle some greyish metal coins, only they weren't coins, they are the Communion Tokens of the Parish. No doubt at all exists who caused them to be made because, there, worn but perfectly legible, each token, about the size of a modern twopenny piece, bears the initial " Mr. W. F." and the date 1795. On the reverse I read " Cor. 11, 28, 29." The really thrilling fact about these venerable pieces of metal lies not only in their antiquity but in the fact that they are still used on Gigha today on each Communion Sunday. I wonder how many churches still use tokens which were presented by communicants nearly two hundred years ago. Imagine presenting a Token which may well have been handled by your great-great-great grandmother or father!

I was still fascinated by this thought when I realised that Mr. Robertson had not come to the end of the treasures of his Parish. From a green baize bag he drew out an enormous leaden plate about a foot or more in diameter. This, he told me, had been the Collection Plate in the days when it was not allowed to take money in the Lord's House. The Elders had to stand outside with it and carry it round to the Vestry at the beginning of the Service. He has seen one in the Highland Church at Campbeltown which has holes in the base, like a sieve to let the rain through so that the coins will not sit in the wet!

Reluctantly I savoured a last feel of Mr. Fraser's Tokens and watched Mr. Robertson put them back in the tin against the next Communion Sabbath, all of whose Services, will be in English. A surprising amount of Gaelic is still spoken on the Island, especially among the older people. The children learn it in School although it is difficult to find a competent teacher as one of the chief difficulties is the pronunciation which bares little relation to the written language as you will gather if you try some of the Gaelic Place names on some of the Gaelic speakers. I find it almost impossible to reproduce the almost lyrical lilt of some of the words. Many of the children understand and can speak a little but writing it is a different matter. I have heard my parents say that, in earlier days, when some of the Islanders spoke only the Gaelic, sending their telegrams was usually dealt with most efficiently by Katie who could not only speak the ancient language but write it, which, in these days was quite an achievement.

By the time I left Mr. Robertson and returned to the road the sun was shining. Everywhere looked sparkling and fresh and I remembered, with a sinking feeling, that this was my last afternoon on the Island. Tomorrow I must return on the *Pioneer* to type out all my notes and have them printed so that everybody could share the thrilling journey into the past of the people of Gigha so that all could appreciate to the full its throbbing life today.

Time for one last walk? But where? Tomorrow, on the way to the Pier I would glimpse Achamore, South Drumachro. Pass the Lodge and stop at New Quay to say good-bye to Sarah. Tonight I would follow my invariable custom. After bidding Katie farewell I'd walk up to Keill past the old Church to watch the sun set in a flaming glory over Islay (it was too late in the season for Jura — that's in the early summer!), drop in on the hospitable cheerful family of McNeills for a last word and finally, as always, drink my final cup of coffee with Susan Orr and Duncan McSporran.

I confess that by the time I'd worked all this out my feet had gone, of their own volition, away towards Tarbert to show you one last treasured place. I always eat the icing of a cake last! Passing the Crofts I waved to one of the lucky people who have come from the Mainland to retire there by the sea where once the kelp workers lived. Drumeonbeg looked down on me from its eyrie on the hillside, where the last of the Galbraiths had farmed. Just before reaching Carnvickoye I went in by a red gate on the right and trudged through the wet grass which Mr. Rennie's cows were munching greedily. Skirting the field with the old Celtic Cross I bore slightly North East towards the sea and found the old disused path I sought. Round a grassy headland I at last came to the sea and, walking briskly down the slope northwards saw before me Highfield the old Garb Acha later Achard and now Highfield. Looking directly over to Kintyre, Highfield must have one of the most gorgeous views of any of the farms. It must also be one of the most exposed. I once asked Angus McVean who had farmed here but has now retired to the Village about this but he just smiled deeply and said " Ach we never noticed that! It was the grandest place to live!"

But I haven't brought you here to see the view or discuss the weather. Here we can see, in its last phase one of the old clachans in process of being turned into a farm, but a farm which never materialised further towards a farmstead. Standing facing the sea a row of stone barns and byres still have inside, remains of the old timbers of the cottages they once were. I counted three and three were occupied in the 1860's but Donald McDonald tells me that, when he was a boy, before the beginning of this century four fishermen's families lived here. At the North end of the group of old cottages stands, apart, a neat white house, which has undoubtedly been fashioned from a cottage. Now it is reverting to a cottage, a modern one, as the farm itself is now worked by Mr. Rennie of Tarbert and the farmhouse is used as a cottage with all modern conveniences. Once these rather tumble-down sheds are demolished the last wraith of the old clachan will have disappeared.

Turning my back on the sea I slithered through the marshy gully along the old road to Highfield. Reaching easier ground I walked over the grass towards Tarbert Bay. Away on my left Neil Bannatyne waved cheerfully as he drove his Tanker back to his old house at Carnvickoye. The day's milk from the Gigha farms was safely up in Achamore ready to be made into Gigha Cheese.

Reaching easier ground I walked over the grass towards Tarbert Bay. Away on my left Neil Bannatyne waved cheerfully as he drove his Tanker back to his old house at Carnvickoye. The day's milk from the Gigha farms was safely up in Achamore ready to be made into Gigha Cheese.

On I went till I looked down on East Tarbert Bay. Down there by the silvery half-moon shaped Bay, if tradition is to be believed, early Christian missionaries landed to visit the Well of St. Breathaig which was just beside me up the hill. In the Field of the Chapel, the *Rudh a Chabeil,* they had set up a church near where the Celtic Cross stands surrounded by the huge stones cleared from around it. Down there, too, at a later date, Norse warriors buried one of their heroes, placing in his grave an exquisite Balance.

In those far-off days the sea encroached further into the land making an even deeper half-moon which is clearly marked by the new grass growing on the sandy crescent where today's farmer has reclaimed ground for his cows' grazing. Here, in this magical place where the seals swim in the clear sea as they have done for centuries, the past meets the present.

Here, then, I take my leave of you for the moment. May you fare well in all your journeys! May the people of Gigha fare well in a continually flourishing Island.

Appendix 1   Some Gigha Place Names

Achavenish — Field of the Narrow Ness.
Achamore — Big Field.
Achnaha — Field of the Kiln.
Ardachy — High Field (on the West).
Achard — High Field (on the East).
Ardminish — Middle Ness.
Aridanleim — Shieling of the Spouting. (See Slocan Leim).

Bagh — A bay.
Belmoir — Big Homestead.
Bodagh and Cailleach — Old man and woman.

Cairnvickoye — ? MacKay's Cairn.
Carn Bhan (pronounced Van) — White Cairn.
Carn na Faire — Watch Cairn.
Cnoc nan Ordag — Hill of Thumbs.
Creag Bhan — White Rock.

Drum — Ridge.
Drumachro — Ridge of the Fold.
Drumeonmore — John's (Eon) Big Ridge.
Drumeonbeg — John's Small Ridge.
Dun Trinsse — Trench Fort.

Eilean — An Island.

Garbacha — Rough Field (later Achard q.v.)
Gigha — (1) Norse gja-ey — Creek or Rift Island.
         (2) Eilean Dhia — God's Island.
         (3) Norse - Gud-ey — God's Island.

Keill (Keills, Kile) — The Cell (Church).
Kile (h) aHan — Cathan's Cell (Church).
Kinerarach — ? Ceann Eararach — East Head.

Leim — see SlocanLeim.

Mull — A Headland.

Port — A Bay.
Port Righ — King's or Chief's Bay.
Port na Galloichille — Galloichille Bay.
Port nan Cuidainnean — Bay of the Cuddies.

Rudh — A Point.
Sgeir-na-hatha — Kiln Rock (Ardminish Bay).
Sgeir-nan-Ron — Seal Rock (off Gigulum).
Tarbert — Isthmus (tarruin - to draw. Bat - a boat).
Tar an Tarb — Loch of the Water Bull.
Tigh — House.
Tigh Creagach — Rock House (Coal Depot).
Tigh Rudh(a) — Point House (E. of Ardminish).
Tobar — a Well.

With acknowledgements to The Kintyre Antiquarian Society's
" Place Names of Gigha and Cara "

Appendix 2   Proprietors (Main Estate)

1797 – John McNeil.

1818 – John McNeil II (Son).

1836 – John Carstairs purchased for son-in-law Alexander McNeill who held till death in 1850.

1850 – John Carstairs McNeill (Son of Alexander).

1865 – J. Williams Scarlett purchased all Gigha.

1880 – William James Scarlett (Son).

1893 – William James Yorke Scarlett (Son).

1919 – Major John Allen (Purchased).

1937 – R. J. A. Hamer (Purchased).

1940 – Somerset de Chair (Wife Elaine Hamer).

1944 – Sir James Horlick (Purchased).

1973 – D. W. Landale (Purchased).

Appendix 3   Ministers (Modern Times)

1717 - 56 – Neil Simpson A.M.

1758 - 84 – Wm. Mowat.

1784 - 89 – Dugald MacDougall.
(1790 – Samuel Peat - never retired).

1794 - 02 – William Fraser A.M.

1803 - 06 – Duncan Rankin.

1807 - 26 – Malcolm Macdonald.

1827 - 77 – James Curdie M.A.

(1869 - 76 – Duncan Black, Asst.).

1877 - 07 – John F. MacKenzie.

1907 - 23 – Donald MacFarlane M.A.

1923 - 48 – Kenneth MacLeod D.D.

1948 - 53 – Angus McMillan.

1954 - 56 – Robert Aitchison.

1957 - 60 – Kenneth Ross (1st term).

1961 - 66 – John G. Ross.

1966 - 70 – Kenneth Ross (2nd term).

1970 - 73 – Vacant. Supply from Killean.

1973 – James Robertson.

Appendix 4   Population Returns – 19th Century
Gigha and Cara

1755 – 514	1831 – 534
1764 – 461	1841 – 550
1771 – 550	1851 – 547
1791 – 614	1861 – 460
1801 – 556	1871 – 390
1811 – 550	1881 – 382
1821 – 574	1891 – 401

Notes

Chapter 1

1. Appendix 1.
2. R. S. G. Anderson. The Antiquities of Gigha (2nd Edition).
3. O.S.A. 54 ft.
4. Argyll. Part 1. Kintyre. No. 13.
5. Op. cit. No. 138.
6. See map on inside front cover.
7. Martin Pennant. A Voyage to the Hebrides. p. 198.
8. Argyll. No. 244.
9. Anderson. p. 126 f.f.
10. Argyll. p. 8 f.f.
11. Op. cit. pp. 16 – 19.
12. Op. cit. No. 164.
13. Op. cit. No. 199.
14. Op. cit. p. 16.
15. Personal letters Mr. J. Philip.
16. Anderson. p. 57; Kintyre Nos. 305/306.
17. Anderson. p. 53 f.f.
18. Argyll. No. 306.
19. Op. cit. No. 245.
20. A group of rocks off the North end from which the nickname comes. Appendix 1.
21. Anderson. p. 16.

Chapter 2

1. The Cathsgeir Light is a black conical Buoy with a white flash every 6 seconds, fitted with a Radar reflector moored in 13 fathoms of water off the West Coast at the end of reed of rocks and a shoal. In June 1905 Mariners were notified that a " Gas-lighted Boat – painted red with a conical superstructure " was about to be erected here. This burnt a special " gas " oil which was taken in tenders from Oban and pumped into the " boat." The illuminant nowadays is " dissolved acetylene gas." I am grateful to the Northern Lighthouse Board for this information.
2. The Story of Gigha. J. MacMaster Campbell. pl.
3. Argyll no. 276.
4. Anderson *op. cit.* p. 85.
5. Dean Munro. 1510. Description of the Western Isles.
6. Martin Martin. A Description of the Western Islands. p. 228.
7. Argyll. No. 276.
8. Anderson. p. 73.
9. Argyll. No. 296.
10. Origines Parochiales. p. 260.
11. Martin *op. cit.* p. 263.

12. Argyll no. 361.
13. T. P. White. Knapdale. p. 384.
14. Anderson *op. cit.* pp. 62 ff.
15. Argyll 276.
16. Anderson *op. cit.* p. 70.
17. Anderson p. 71.
18. Appendix 2.
19. Hew Scott. Fasti Ecclesiae Scoticanae 1923.
20. Anderson p. 87.

Chapter 3

1. To avoid peppering this chapter with numbers, to the detriment of pleasurable reading, I add that most of the detailed information herein is taken from *Originales Parochiales* published by the Scotae Bannatyne Club Ed. 1851. pp. 257 ff.
   Anderson and J. MacMaster Campbell have taken their information from it. The difficulty is that, since its publication, the McNeill Charters have been lost and, so far no other documentary source has been found. From now on a valuable source of information are the Estate Papers which are deposited in the present Proprietor's Solicitor's Office in Edinburgh and I am very grateful to Mr. Landale for allowing me free access to these original deeds. Otherwise the best short general History is that by J. D. Mackie published by Pelican.
2. J. MacMaster Campbell. p. 13.
3. Estate Papers.
4. Anderson p. 16.
5. Dean Munro, Description of the Western Isles.
6. Estate Papers.
7. J. MacMaster Campbell. p. 15.
8. Estate Papers.

Chapter 4

Except where elsewhere indicated the information in this chapter is from the Estate papers. (Notes (1) Scoull = later New Quay and Duntro appears in both Estates under different tenants. Following up the tenancies reveals that South Drumachro was in the Main Estate. (2) A merkland is an old Scottish measure of distance. It varies from place to place and is not accurately measureable).

1. O.S.A. p. 63.
2. Anderson. p. 84.
3. O.S.A. p. 41 n.
4. N.S.A. p. 400.
5. Seven Centuries. A History of the Lockharts of Lee and Carnwath by Simon MacDonald Lockhart published by the Author at the Estate Office, Carnwath, Lanarkshire. This fascinating book has a valuable chapter on the MacDonalds of Largie.

Chapter 5

1. James Hunter. The Making of the Crofting Community. p. 76.
2. A. B. B. Haldane. The Drove Roads of Scotland. p. 57
3. Haldane op. cit. p. 50.
4. Haldane op. cit. p. 95.
5. J. MacMaster Campbell. op. cit. p. 13; Anderson p. 76.
6. Chapter 8.
7. Argyll Papers. Bundle 600.

Chapter 6

1. Several meetings were held at South Drumachro.
2. Kinerarach.
3. Highfield.
4. Carnvickoye.
5. As Mhullian means Mill I think this is one of the Ardailly farms.
6. Shensrioch is discussed at length in Chapter 7 p.
7. " The report," the record noted " came in a letter to the Minister."
8. Besides our debt to J. M. Ross I owe a good deal of this information to the Reverend Ian Muirhead, until recently Lecturer in Ecclesiastical History at Glasgow University.
9. Ross. p. 20 onwards.

Chapter 7

1. New Statistical Account. 1845.
2. Above Chapter 4. p. 39 f.f.
3. Letter to Author from J. Aikman Smith Esq.. Secretary, West Highland Steamer Club. Much of the information supplied by G. E. Langmuir, author of West Highland Steamers.
4. Estate Papers.
5. The mother was affectionately known as Ellie Mhor (Big Ellie) and the daughter as Ellie B haig pronounced Vaic) — little Ellie.
6. James Hunter op. cit. 19.
7. Appendix. 4.
8. Napier Commission Report 1865.
9. James Hunter op. cit. pp. 29.
10. Below end of this chapter. Map on Inside cover.
11. Anderson.
12. Particularly at Ardlammy and Achamore.
13. The name signifies the Purse-bearer and is often rendered as Pursell or Purseworth.

Chapter 8

1. The Album is now the property of the Author. Copies of most of the Photographs adorn the walls of Gigha Hotel.
2. W. W. Philip subsequently became a J.P. and an F.S.I. For many years on the Council of the Clydesdale Horse Society, he served for a time as its President. He also wrote several pamphlets on Agriculture.

3. O.S.A. p. 68.
4. Sarah is the widow of a son of William McSporran.
5. A rich fruit pudding cooked in a cloth.
6. Several people by tradition recited poetry — the Factor " Aye gave us Tam o' Shanter, the whole o' it."
7. Jenny, now Mrs. McKellar. The Andrew Family moved to Renfrewshire where many of them still farm. Although not mentioned by name in the text Marianne, born at Leim and now Mrs. John Mackie, has been tireless in providing valuable information.
8. The present Author.

Chapter 9

1. One of the most revealing and interesting facts about Gigha life today is that the population of just over 150 have raised over £10,000 in two years for the Church and Manse Fund. This has involved a truly communal effort of men, women and children.